DR. ROMANCE™'S GUIDE
TO
FINDING LOVE TODAY

BY

TINA B. TESSINA, Ph.D.

Order this title at http://www.tinatessina.com

Library of Congress Cataloging-in-Publication Data
Tessina, Tina B.
Dr. Romance™'s Guide to Finding Love Today
ISBN-13: 978-1722976415
ISBN-10: 1722976411
BISAC: FAM: 051000 **FAMILY & RELATIONSHIPS** / Dating

1. Relationships. 2. Dating 3. Self-Help I. Title.

For My Single Friends and Clients

Let's make your dreams of love come true.

ACKNOWLEDGMENTS

To my husband, Richard Sharrard: Sweetheart, sharing life and love with you since 1982 has been a great joy. Thank you for all your love, your sense of humor, and your support and understanding.

To my dynamic agent and friend Laurie Harper, who has supported me through all the ups and downs of this crazy business of writing books. Thank you for all your advice, encouragement, and very practical help, and for friendship far beyond the role of an agent.

Yet another salute to my chosen family, in (more or less) alphabetical order: Isadora Alman and Morton Chalfy, Maggie and Ed Bialack, Victoria Bryan, Sylvia and Glen McWilliams, David Groves, Bobbi Palmer and Riley K. Smith. Each of you really knows what friends are for, and I am surrounded by love, laughter, and caring because of you.

TABLE OF CONTENTS

INTRODUCTION

Finding Love Today

You are reading Dr. Romance's guide for one of several reasons: you want to find love, you're recently out of a relationship, or you're contemplating a change. Whichever reason fits, if it's been a while since you last dated, or if you think you could improve your odds, you need facts, techniques and answers. The following chapters will cover all the basics, some things you already know, and many things you never thought of.

If you are not currently married, you are certainly not alone.

According to the U.S. Census Bureau Profile America Facts for Features, July 30, 2013:

- There were 103 million unmarried people in America 18 and older in 2012, which is 44.1 percent of all U.S. residents 18 and older. 53.6% were women and 46.4 percent were men.

- 62% of the unmarried U.S. residents 18 and older had never been married. Another 24 percent were divorced, and 14 percent were widowed, and 46% of households were maintained by unmarried men and women in 2012.

- 33 million people lived alone in 2012, which is up ten percent since 1970, and they comprise 27 percent of all households. Unmarried U.S. residents 65 and older make up 16 percent of all unmarried people 18 and older.

While (and to an extent, because) the number of unmarried people has risen dramatically, social mores have also changed drastically. Women and men both have far freedom and opportunity today for creating their lives and relationships than in the mid-20th Century, and, as we have seen endlessly in the media, there is a much more relaxed attitude toward sexuality, living together, relationships and courtship.

These dramatic changes have been accompanied by equally dramatic shifts in what we expect from relationships, how long they last, and how we find them. So, if it's been any length of time since you last dated, there are a lot of changes you need to know about; as well as what is the same in human relationships.

The Changes in Technology

The flood of new innovative technology today can be overwhelming. It has impacted lifestyles, relationships and every social interaction. Dating and socializing are drastically changed from what was happening in the eighties and nineties. Whether you are tech savvy or tech resistant, Dr. Romance™ will help you negotiate the brave new world of finding love today.

Your Dating Experience

Perhaps you never expected to be dating at this point, but, like so many others today, you are unexpectedly on your own, and you don't know where to begin. Or, you've been dating for a long time, and can't seem to find a good match. Whether you have just had a relationship breakup, a divorce, your partner or spouse recently passed away, or you have simply not been dating for a while, you can find what you need here: the information you need to find suitable people to date, a clear and effective process to follow, the current attitudes and relationship etiquette, and the know-how to feel confident about your social skills.

For many years, dating was something done by young people, during high school or college, and the expectation was that they would find partners and settle down before too long. With all the social and technological changes of the new millennium, more people than ever are waiting longer to marry, and/or becoming single later in life. Today, the dating phase has been extended into adulthood, middle age and even the senior years. You might be divorced or a single parent with small or adult children. Whatever stage of life you are in, if you want to find love today, this is the book for you.

Since you are not a teenager, you have the benefit of much more life experience. The positive thing about this is you already have learned a lot of social and relationship skills that will be very helpful in finding the love you want. On the other hand, there can be a downside to experience. If you have lost a previous relationship, you may have *baggage:* leftover anger, hurt, fear or grief that will cause you to react differently in the next relationship. Baggage can also be left over from a difficult family situation or a poor self-image. In these pages, you can learn how to unpack your baggage, resolve old fears and problems, and get a fresh start at love and life.

Finding a Date Today

Everyone has some trouble figuring out how to meet suitable people. It's a common problem. You are probably not often in an environment that automatically surrounds you with eligible dates. Even if you are, dating people from your work and your neighborhood can present problems. Clubs, workshops and social activities aren't always the most successful places to go, and online dating forums and apps present their own unique set of challenges. We'll cover the pros and cons of all these options in Chapter Six: Successful Searching.

To date successfully today, you need well-thought out plans and strategies that work. You could learn from experience, but you've probably tried that, and found it's time-consuming to learn to date by trial and error, and not very successful. Here you'll learn what strategies have the best odds of success, and how to develop one that suits your personality and circumstances.

Why Are You Dating?

Whether you are a young adult, a single parent, a widow/er or a senior and have experienced loss, or even if you have given up on relationships or spent years alone, this guide will tell you what you need to know to draw on your own life experience and expertise and apply those skills to the dating process. It is very difficult to begin looking for love after the loss of a beloved spouse. The grief and disorientation associated with being widowed can make the whole thought of dating seem impossible. Here you will find out how to complete your healing and move on into a comfortable connection with new people.

- If you're just out of an immersive environment such as school and wondering how you meet people in the big, wide, world this book will show you how and where to meet people you can actually enjoy meeting and learn something about.

- If you are looking for love as a result of a difficult ending to your previous relationship, such as a divorce or an acrimonious breakup, you can learn how to avoid repeating old mistakes.

- If you're a single parent, you'll learn when and how to introduce a new date to your children, and how to handle the reactions of both your children and your date.

- If you're dating a single parent, you'll learn the best ways to cope with the sometimes complicated dynamics of dating someone who has children.

- If you fear that you are too old to begin searching for love now, you'll find appropriate, dignified and fun ways to open up to new experiences with old friends and new connections.

Sometimes relationship experiences can be so difficult that you may have given up on relationships altogether, thinking that living alone is your lot in life. If you are not completely happy with this choice, we can show you how to come out of isolation and make a new, much more successful start. If your isolation has covered a span of years, opening up to new experiences can be frightening. The information, facts and guidelines we have collected for you here can get you past your fear and into a more satisfying social life. *Dr. Romance*™*'s Guide to Finding Love Today* covers all the basic information you need to know to successfully re-start your search.

What you can learn from this book:

- What to do with the baggage from your past
- How to find the right kind of person for you
- Etiquette for today
- How to handle friends, roommates, parents, & children
- What to do if it becomes a relationship
- What to do if it doesn't work out
- What to do the night before
- What to do the morning after
- What to say in person or on the phone
- How to handle social media
- How dating sites and apps work, and how to use them.

No matter which of these issues you need to know about, or what questions you have, you'll find the answers in here are timely, helpful and fit the world you face as a single person dating today.

CHAPTER ONE

A Challenge and an Adventure

Does this sound familiar? The thought of finding love is exciting, and you spend time fantasizing about it, perhaps even about certain people you've seen around, but every time you think of actually doing something about it, you're terrified. The few things you have actually done, blind dates set up by friends, swiping a dating app, meeting someone in a club, attending a singles event or (horrors) trying to date your ex again have all been awful, which increases the fear factor. You need some help!

Your fears are understandable. They are created by the prevalent fantasy about dating: You and some person you don't know will meet, make an instant, 100% accurate evaluation of each other, decide to go out, and spend an evening together falling in love.

No wonder that's scary: it may happen in the movies, but it's just plain impossible in a real life like yours. If you have ever expected that to be true, you have probably had some miserable evenings. You just don't know enough about the other person at first sight to declare your interest and guarantee that extended, one-on-one contact will be pleasant. There have to be better ways to accomplish meeting and getting to know people.

Learning to socialize as a single adult

You may not have thought about it this way, but finding love takes knowhow, and the various skills it requires have to be learned somewhere. You can learn them by trial-and-error, but that's painful and time-consuming. Unlike teenagers, you don't have a lot of time to spend fantasizing, giggling in corners, and making lots of mistakes. And meeting strangers in the grown-up world can even be dangerous. The good news is, there's a technology of dating that works; and it makes meeting new people easy, fun and successful. That's what this guide is about.

Are You Feeling Lost and Inadequate?

It may have been OK, when you were 13, to feel inadequate and miserable (although I'll you didn't enjoy it then, either), but at least everyone else you knew felt about the same. And no one expected much of you then, anyway. Things are different today. Not only is dating something you haven't practiced for a while (or maybe a very long time), but so much more is expected of an adult in today's world. It's easy to feel you're competing with movie stars, models, and smooth characters in TV sitcoms, who usually wind up with a date in the end.

In your own mind, you probably are comparing yourself (or your date) to:
- Whoever made People Magazine's "Sexiest Man Alive"
- The amazing stars on the Red Carpet
- Benedict Cumberbatch, everyone's favorite "Sherlock"
- Princess Kate Middleton, gorgeous new mom
- Kate's dashing husband, Prince William
- Meghan Markle, the actress who became a princess
- Angelina Jolie, Oscar winner, movie star and philanthropist
- Beyoncé Knowles singer and beauty icon
- Ben Affleck, versatile movie star and heartthrob
- Reese Witherspoon, the most frequent star in romance comedies
- Katy Perry, ground-breaking rocker

- Julianne Hough, blonde beauty who went from *Dancing with the Stars* to being a star
- Brad Pitt, handsome husband of Jolie
- Leonardo DiCaprio, the rags-to-tuxedo heartthrob from *Titanic*

These stars, (or whoever is on your own list) benefit from lighting, scripts, makeup, direction, cosmetic surgery, costuming, and constant retouching; which we never think of, when comparing ourselves. Sometimes, in fact, we get a glimpse of their ordinary side in the tabloids, in grubby clothes, with wild hair, looking more like we do.

And, on the inside, the idols we mentally compete with are as insecure, confused and imperfect as we are. For example, we had a glimpse into mega-success Dustin Hoffman, a happily married man, and his moments of self-doubt when he burst into tears on the American Film Institute's "100 Years of Great Movies" TV special, as he was interviewed about "Tootsie" because he said the role (cross-dressed and not beautiful) put him in touch with how many intelligent women he has ignored, because they weren't attractive. And the many tragic suicides and drug- addiction problems indicate these celebrities may not be as happy as we'd like to believe.

Baggage: Haunted by Old Mistakes and Bad Experiences

Although you might think of "falling in love" as a one-time romantic event, we all fall in love many times in life: with a new lover, a new friend, a particularly cooperative and friendly co-worker, an appealing movie or TV star, a caring mentor, siblings, relatives and beloved pets. Any close relationship involves falling in love at least a little bit, and it's these connections that make life pleasurable.

10 Reasons for Not Falling in Love

But, sometimes making connections becomes scary, and you feel the need to protect yourself instead of reaching out with an open heart. I see many clients who have trouble connecting with others, making enjoyable friendships, and have struggles with family members, so they experience relationships of all types as difficult and painful. There are many reasons people hold back and remain closed off. Holding back and resisting caring can cause you to become overcommitted to certain relationships (co-dependent), too clingy in others, or to appear cold and standoffish. Emotional trauma from childhood and past relationships is called baggage, because it's extra stuff carried into all your relationships, which effects how you perceive your interactions.

Here are ten reasons you may not feel comfortable being open and available for love:

1. You've been burned before: If you got hurt or disappointed in a prior relationship, you might be reluctant to take another risk.

2. Shyness: Being afraid of meeting new people will hold you back from meeting the person you can fall in love with. No matter how cool you may be in your business dealings, with your friends, or in front of strangers you don't want to date, if you're contemplating meeting people to date, you may stammer, get tongue tied, blush, fidget, look at everything but the person, your heart may race, and you can find yourself breaking out in all kinds of mannerisms that remind you of being a teen.

3. Holding out for Mr. or Ms. Right: If you reject everyone who seems less than perfect at first glance, you might reject the very one you could fall in love with, if you got to know their finer qualities.

4. Growing up in a dysfunctional family: Growing up with parents who fought a lot or were angry, cold or violent; or with a divorced or single parent who couldn't develop relationships that lasted can leave you without a skill set for

finding and making a connection with a healthy person 5. Sex too soon: Having sex right away changes your connection from possible relationship to one-night stand. You can cease to be a person in your date's eyes, and just become a booty call.

5. Body image issues: If you're too self-critical about your body and your look, you may be so self-obsessed that you never even notice when someone else likes you, and you miss your chance.

6. Sexual hang-ups: if you're too focused on sex, or too repressed about it, you'll be reluctant to allow intimacy and love to grow.

7. Violent history: If you were in a previous violent relationship, you'll have PTSD that will stop you from taking another risk.

8. Low self-confidence: If you're not comfortable with yourself, you won't allow others to get close and discover you.

9. Still Grieving: If you haven't recovered from your last relationship, it's too soon to let someone else in. I've seen many people in my office who say they don't want another relationship, or even a pet, because losing the last one hurt too much.

Seeing Through New Eyes

No matter how well prepared you are, every new relationship will be unique. Some will obviously be better than others. The whole point of meeting new people is to get to know them and let them discover you. Since everyone you meet will be a unique individual, there's no way to be completely prepared for what will happen. Every new relationship is a surprise and a mystery. If you are prepared to learn and to be surprised, seeking to control only your own responses, and prepared to make realistic plans and decisions, you'll enjoy most of the experience. Caring means venturing into the unknown, exploring and learning, so enjoy the adventure, and you'll get the best results.

If you are an adult, you have a lot of life experience, sometimes called baggage. Some of your experience will be helpful, and some will be problematic. If you take the time to examine your history and experience, you'll find you've learned a lot, and when you learn from a loss or a mistake, you grow your emotional repertoire, and I think it's how we grow our souls. The skill you've learned in your life, in work, with friends, in team sports and social events, and at school can be very helpful in all your relationships, if you understand that you can transfer other life skills to the dating situation. If you hire and/or manage people in your job, for example, use the intuitive skill you've developed there to scope out someone you've just met. Without being obvious, you can interview this person, and draw out information. If what you hear would make you want to hire him or her, then a friendship might be a good experience.

Beginning (or even contemplating) a relationship activates these memories, and brings your old fears and insecurities to the surface. Old issues have not been resolved such as fear of abandonment, fear of intimacy, fear of rejection; will surface to be cleared away. For example, if you had a competitive relationship with your siblings, you may find yourself competing with other people in inappropriate ways. Once you learn, very early in life, that relationships, (including with your original family, childhood friendships, teenage friendships or adult relationships) don't happen automatically, and problems can come up, especially emotionally painful problems; it's very easy to become phobic, or intensely afraid, of being hurt or rejected.

To overcome the fear, you need to learn to look at your relationships in a new way. You can 'meet' people you already know; even family members, by looking at them differently. Instead of thinking about your parent, sibling or extended family member in the same old way, try meeting them anew, as you would a stranger, and finding out who they are apart from what you already know. Asking a family member about their history before you were born, or an experience they had that you were not part of will give you a new perspective.

Because each new person is a new experience, you probably feel out of control; and you are. There is no way to control what will happen, or how the other person will act or respond. However, you are always in control of your own actions and responses, and that can make a vast difference in how your friendships and relationships progress. If you keep in mind that you get to choose what you say and do, and it's about enjoying the other person, not pleasing them, you'll have better results. Prior pain is often a reason why people dread a new experience. If your history of relationships has been painful, hurtful or a disaster; it's natural not to want to try it again. However, it's worth a try, because even one good relationship experience can help heal the hurts from the past relationships that did not work out.

Relationships cause you to grow emotionally, which can be a bit scary. If you keep in mind, however, that the new self you are creating will be happier, more socially confident, and very likely happier, you can overcome reluctance and get enthused. You will actually be able to relax, and have a good time. In addition to feeling one-down because you can't live up to a mega-star image, you may be suffering some wounds from past relationship problems. Relationships that don't last, especially the ones that end badly, or that were painful, can undermine your self-confidence (especially if it was not too solid to begin with) and make you reluctant to try again. Even a wonderful relationship which ended only because your partner died can be scarring. Bonding with someone is risky, because there's always a possibility you might have to go through the searing pain of loss, or the terrible ordeal of watching your beloved die, while you stand by helpless.

Once you've suffered problems, pain and loss like this, it takes great courage to begin all over again. This guide will help you recover from your past pain and loss, and gain the courage to bounce back and try again. Whatever route brought you here, you are contemplating finding love today, and that means you're at least feeling ready enough to think about it.

Does Looking for Love Seem Fearsome to You?
The next hurdle you'll encounter is figuring out how dating (that social milieu known only to the uncoupled) works, and what you must do to succeed. As adults, we are used to being in charge, and pretty competent in most of the things we do. Plunging into a new dynamic undermines this competence: beginners are, by definition, not good at what they're doing. This can be daunting, and the solution is to allow yourself to have what the Zen Buddhists call a beginner's mind. "If your mind is empty, it is always ready for anything;" teaches Zen Master Shunryu Suzuki in *Zen to Go*, "it is open to everything. In the beginner's mind there are many possibilities, but in the expert's there are few."

Allowing yourself be in a learning mode, to be a beginner at dating, gives you several advantages:

- You can be open to new experiences
- No pressure to be perfect the first time
- You might invent a new, better way of doing something
- You can more easily correct old, bad habits

How to Use Beginner's Mind
- *You Can Take Your Time:* Being a beginner, new to dating (this time around, anyway), means you can take it slowly, allowing yourself to scope out what others are doing, and learning by the examples (good and bad) of those around you. When you are in learning mode, you are more alert, pay more attention, and actually experience more than if you are operating by a tried and true, set system. The tentative feeling of being in a new situation helps you to be alert to things you wouldn't otherwise notice. For example, in a dance club for the first time, if you're worried about looking attractive and knowledgeable, you'll be focusing on what everyone thinks of you. But, if you

are intending to learn, your attention will be on what others are doing, and you'll evaluate how successful everyone's approach is. Try it, and you'll see how having a beginner's mind works: The first time in a new singles event, club, or situation, don't expect to meet anyone. Go with the intention of observing, and watch what goes on from a comfortable corner. You'll be more relaxed, and you'll get a better feel for the culture of the place.

- *No pressure to be perfect the first time:* As a beginner, if you make a mistake, it will feel like less of a tragedy. Beginners don't have to impress anyone with anything other than their openness to learn. Be willing to say to people you meet, "I'm new at this". If you are coming out of a previous relationship it will be seen as an asset, as in: "This person knows how to have a relationship!" Also, being "the new kid on the block" motivates others to be helpful, and to show you the ropes. You are not a threat or a challenge when you're a beginner.

- *You might invent a new, better way of doing something:* Many of the world's great inventions were mistakes made by someone fumbling around with the unknown. Modern rubber, for example, was invented in 1839 when Charles Goodyear accidentally spilled some of a concoction he was cooking onto a stove. Who knows what naive mistakes you can make that will revolutionize dating, at least for you? Don't be afraid to get a little creative: if it fails, you'll have something to laugh about, and if it succeeds, you might get very lucky.

- *You can more easily correct old, bad habits:* Opening up your mind to learning new things makes it easier to bypass old, automatic behavior. "Every situation we face in life is different," writes Harvard learning researcher Dr. Ellen Langer, author of *Mindfulness* "and learning from each one requires.... mindful learning, which involves taking in new

14

information in a way that allows us to use it in different situations....to vary the basics to allow each of us to use our unique physical skills, mental abilities and personalities to the fullest."

Trying new things, playing with the situation, and making it fun for yourself could lead to making a mistake, but it is more likely to make the experience more interesting, and teach you something you need to know.

Putting Yourself on the Line

Part of what's so intimidating about trying to meet someone is that, the minute you get interested in someone, no matter how casually, you're exposing yourself to the possibility of rejection. In fact, one of the techniques taught in many how to date workshops is to try and get rejected as many times as possible. This little mental trick makes getting rejected the goal, so either you're meeting your goal, or you don't get rejected; thus turning the process into a win/win situation. If you decide to embrace getting rejected, be careful not to overdo it. You don't want to create extra rejection for yourself where it wouldn't otherwise exist. Trying to get rejected simply means to be open to meeting as many people as possible, and introducing yourself, even if you think you might be rejected.

"Does he (or she) like me?" Is the first question most of us would ask upon being attracted to someone, but it's much more appropriate to ask yourself, "Do I like him or her?" What this new person thinks of you is his or her responsibility, not yours. Your job is to find out what you think about this stranger. There will be many more techniques for how to do this in later chapters. In today's atmosphere of changing roles and lifestyles, things can get confusing. The key to these problems is to know what message each approach sends, so you can choose what impression you're making. How to make conversation, body language and social skills are all skills you'll learn in the following chapters.

Does approaching strangers make you feel unsure and incompetent? When you take the risk of approaching a stranger, to try and get to know him or her better (or when someone approaches you) you encounter that beginner feeling again. No matter how cool you may be in your workplace, with your friends, or in front of other strangers, when you meet a person you may want to date, you may stammer, get tongue tied, blush, fidget, look at everything but the person, your heart may race, and you can find yourself breaking out in all kinds of mannerisms that remind you of being a teen. Psychologists call this *regression:* feeling younger than your actual age. It happens under stress, in new situations, and when some problem from your childhood seems to be repeating itself. In this case, what you're regressing to is a childlike hunger for approval and acceptance. Take this in stride, and remember your beginner's mind: you'll be anxious for the first few times, and then you'll calm down. After a couple of successful connections with the people around you (nothing more than friendly smiles or hello's), you'll find you begin to feel more like your normal self, and your fear will transform itself into excitement, which is much more fun.

How to Talk to a Potential Date for The First Time
- Remind yourself not to run negative comparisons about some screen idol or super model image, and that neither you nor this other person is super human. You are both just people, and the other person may feel as unsure and nervous as you do.
- Take a slow breath, and take your time.
- Smile.
- Look over the other person to become aware of what has caught your interest: perhaps it's what he or she is wearing, a nice accessory or smartwatch, a lovely smile, striking blue eyes, a pretty color of hair or clothing.
- Say "Hello", or respond to whatever he or she says
- Give a compliment, and

- Ask a question, like: "That's a striking pendant you're wearing. Does it have a special meaning?" Or "My, your eyes are an amazing color. Does it run in your family?" Or, "I would like to get a smartwatch like yours, do you like it?" It will get your conversation off and running.

Even though you risk making some mistakes, feeling a little foolish, being disappointed at times, and being rejected a few times, when you do it right, looking for love (in the right places) can be a lot of fun. Finding the right person to date, and hopefully even fall in love with, is worth taking a few risks. As they say in aerobics, "no pain, no gain."

You can learn to maximize your fun and minimize your difficulties with a little information, some pointers and some careful planning. What can make dating miserable is blundering around, without a plan, and learning by trial and error. Those unplanned errors can be very painful and costly! The risk involved in dating should be well-thought-out and planned for, so the consequences aren't too drastic. Every chance you take should have pretty good odds of being successful, and the worst you'll experience will be minor emotional discomfort. This guide shows you how to maximize the fun, and minimize the mistakes.

The Risks

Dating, especially if you are not used to it, presents three possible types of risk:

- emotional pain
- financial expense
- physical risk

One of the aims of this guide is to teach you how to avoid each type of risk. We live in a very mobile society, which makes it easy for people to be dishonest about who they are and their intentions toward you. Treat your emotions, your body and your money as equally precious, and don't give control of any of them to another person until you are sure you have taken care of your safety.

- *Emotional pain:* When you know your vulnerable areas, take the time to find out who the other person is, and go slowly into commitment. For example, if, for you, sexual intercourse is equal to commitment or being exclusive of other partners, it's very important that you make sure what having sex means to your partner before you go ahead. Or, if you're seeing someone who becomes critical of you, or wants to take advantages of you, pull back until you find out what's going on. Slowing down is the best way to avoid a painful situation.

- *Financial expense:* It's smart to budget your dating expenses, and stay within the limits, managing them just as you manage the rest of your finances. Don't let the excitement of a new connection or the desire to impress tempt you to spend more than you can afford. Making financial commitments takes as much careful checking as making sexual and emotional commitments.

- *Physical risk:* We all hope dating will be romantic and have a happy ending, but any newscast will show you that it can be dangerous. Protect yourself by meeting new people only in public places, at a local coffee house for a chat) by being alert to the signs of dangerous people presented in this book, (reckless driving, drinking too much, angry outbursts, too controlling) and, of course, by protecting your health with safer sex practices. Don't hesitate to cyber-stalk a potential relationship: Facebook, Pinterest and other Internet sites can reveal a lot about a potential relationship, and so can an Internet search. Even if you meet through an Internet dating site that promises to vet members, don't assume they do. Their checks can be very superficial, and easily gotten around by someone who has bad intentions.

For example:

- Emotional safety: Don't let yourself fall in love with someone until you have followed the guidelines in this book to make sure that person is genuine.
- Physical safety: Don't let someone else drive you unless you're sure they're not drinking. Practice safer sex.
- Financial safety: Don't loan money, or sign financial papers because you are in love. Financial entanglements cloud relationships.

Many guidelines for personal safety are included in the chapters of this book. By following them, you can minimize the dangers of dating, and maximize your fun.

Who's in control

Most people feel more comfortable being in control of the situations they're in, so much so, that we often pretend we're in control when we're really not, or try to control situations that we cannot reasonably handle. Remember, you are never in control of another person, even if it seems that you are, and that they wish you to be. You can't control who you'll meet, when or where you'll meet them, their feelings, their ethics and motivation, or their actions.

Self-control is the only real control you have. However, it is all the control you'll need. By taking responsibility for your own actions, words, and reactions, you can greatly stack the odds in your own favor. I think of responsibility as *response-ability*: the ability to respond to life, people and events. While you may not be responsible for most of what happens, you are completely responsible for your reaction to what is happening.

For example, if you are out with a new person and that person acts in some frightening or unacceptable manner, you have the ability to respond in many ways:

- You can react without thinking, and perhaps make the situation worse,

- If things get unpleasant or threatening, you can leave (even if it means paying for a ride-hailing service like Uber or Lyft, a cab, or leaving your date in a restaurant),
- You can ask someone (such as the restaurant manager) for help. You can also respond by deciding not to date that person again, even if feelings have been developing in the relationship. Being responsible means taking care of yourself, even if it's difficult.
- Or, if you find that your date likes to tempt you to drink more alcohol, you can exercise your self-control and limit your drinking to a level that's acceptable to you, even if your date complains that you're no fun.

Learning as You Go, Mistakes Are Ok
Dating is just another learning process. You have learned a lot in your life: how to dress appropriately, how to drive, how to use a new phone or tablet, how to play tennis. This is no different. It's a series of skills and information you can master, with some practice, as you have other skills. Cartoonist Matt Groening, creator of "The Simpsons" had a difficult time learning to date. "I didn't know anything about love back then. I was completely screwed up on the subject. I'd had a few relationships here and there, but for some reason they kept blowing up in my face. I couldn't figure it out.... I had no money. I barely scraped together my rent every month by cartooning.... This was not as glamorous as it sounds. ...A few women did agree to go out with me anyway, but they didn't last too long. Sooner or later I'd show up at their apartments, ready for another cheap night out, and they'd say the meanest, most vicious things you can say to another person. Things like: 'We have to talk'" But he learned. He and his first wife Deborah were married for 13 years, and he got remarried in 2011.

Common dating mistakes today
- *Trying to be cool:* Don't expect to be ms/mr cool. The imaginary image of what's fashionable is another of those

frightening fantasies, like the model/movie idol. Since such trends are driven by a combination of advertising, mimicking social outcasts and personal creativity. It's difficult to keep current on them.

- *Too Trendy:* While Goth, Grunge, very revealing and Red Carpet styles may be popular, they are also extreme and will limit your success in the dating process. They also send a message about who you are that may not be accurate.
- *Sloppy dressing:* Even though our sex symbol/movie stars are going through a period of various grunge or unkempt looks, those looks are carefully contrived, and a result of extra grooming, not a lack of it. To be successful at dating, you need to be well groomed. Even the trend toward casual clothes is misleading, because that look is as carefully contrived as any formal or business outfit.

Looking good is important, and takes some effort. Being well groomed is much more effective than being cool. You may need to tap some resources (like a stylish friend who always looks good) to get some help with your look, or take some selfies and see for yourself.

Stepping into the Unknown:
No matter how well prepared you are, every dating experience will be unique. Some will obviously be better than others. The whole point of dating is to meet new people, and get to know them. In the process, you are likely to make some friends of both genders, and to have a lot of interesting experiences. Since everyone you meet will be a unique individual, there's no way to be completely prepared for what will happen. What will happen is a surprise. If you allow yourself to experience each date with a beginner's mind, prepared to learn and to be surprised, seeking to control only your own responses, and prepared to make realistic plans and decisions, you'll enjoy most of the experience.

If you accept that dating is venturing into the unknown, exploring and learning, you will be in the best possible frame of mind, able to enjoy the adventure and you'll get the best results.

Unpacking Your Baggage

As we mentioned in the introduction, if you are an adult, and not dating for the very first time, you have a lot of life experience and baggage. Some of your experience will be helpful, and some will be problematic. If you take the time to examine your history and experience, you'll find you've learned a lot. The skill you've learned in your life, in work, with friends, in team sports and social events, and at school can be very helpful in meeting new dates. Many people, especially if they're nervous about dating, don't realize they can transfer other life skills to the situation.

You can use your life experience, such as business skills, to improve the odds of success. If you hire and/or manage people in your job, for example, use the intuitive skill you've developed there to scope out the person you've just met. Without being obvious, you can interview this person, and draw out information. If what you hear would make you want to hire him or her, then a date might be a good experience. On the other hand, some of your life experiences have probably been painful, and that may add some problems.

The Baggage of Your Past

Emotional traumas we bring with us from childhood and past relationships is called baggage, because it's extra stuff we carry with us into all our relationships, which effects how we perceive our relationship interactions. Beginning (or even contemplating) a relationship activates these memories, and brings your old fears and insecurities to the surface. Old issues have not been resolved; such as fear of abandonment, fear of intimacy, fear of rejection, will surface to be cleared away. "...a relationship," author/ psychologist Ken Keyes has written "is like a mirror right there at the tip of your nose. It constantly reflects.... your stuff." Even though this may feel like a problem when it happens, it isn't. It's an opportunity to prevent your relationship problems from reoccurring. Unpacking this baggage can keep it from causing you to repeat your old patterns in these new relationships.

A Course in Emotional Growth

Here is a helpful way to think about dating and relationship problems, which will make focusing on solutions easier, and increase the odds that your relationships will improve. You may not think of it this way, but the most successful way to find love today is to see it as a course in emotional growth. You are probably quite practiced in taking courses. If you sign up for an algebra course, for example, you know what you'll face: ten (or so) weeks of learning new material and homework assignments consisting of more and more complex problems based on the material learned. You may grumble about the homework load, or complain about the teacher, but you never think you've been given the problems as punishment. Problems are a natural part of the educational process.

Life is also a classroom with many classes. One of the most rigorous courses is Love 101. It's required, no one escapes it, and the skills learned are useful for an entire lifetime. The syllabus for this class includes love of self, family, and friends. The advanced syllabus includes love of enemies and those who disappoint, hurt or frustrate us. All of the problems presented are to help us stretch and grow emotionally. Every relationship you have is a learning lesson in love, both of yourself and of the other. When you keep in mind you are a student, and problems are to learn from, you will make your life easier, grow faster, and everything will make more sense.

To handle problems with grace and ease, try responding with the following steps:

1. Be aware of your internal reaction. Are you anxious, angry, worried, startled?
2. Look for what you can learn about the problem: What is really going on?
3. If your date has a problem or is upset, say "tell me more"

23

4. Listen carefully
5. Don't focus on who's at fault; focus on what will fix the problem.

If you approach every relationship issue, whether it's your internal fears or a problem with your date, as a learning opportunity, you'll find that you and your date both stay calmer, and the problem can usually be fixed without a struggle.

Why am I so afraid?
Once you learn, very early in life, that relationships, (including those with your original family, childhood friendships, teenage romances or adult relationships) don't happen automatically, and problems can come up, especially emotionally painful problems, it's very easy to become reactive, irrational or intensely afraid of being hurt or rejected. To overcome the fear, you need to learn to look at your dating relationships in a new way.

You have already learned about several techniques for taking care of yourself:

- Having a beginner's mind
- seeking to learn,
- paying attention to the character flaws and assets of the other person,
- keeping your distance from hurtful people
- taking responsibility for your actions and responses

In the chapters that follow, you'll learn more details about these techniques and more, plus useful information and tips to eliminate fear and pain and make your dating experience fun.

If this is such fun, why do I dread it?
The fun of dating and romance is misrepresented by movies, TV, commercials and other media. From these representations, it appears that love is for beautiful people, and the scenes depicted often have a hyperactive quality that looks attractive on the surface, but feels subtly scary. You recognize that such a high level of

energy would not feel comfortable in real life. Coupled with past painful experiences, that may contradict the fun image, and feel more like misery. If you feel that way, it's natural to approach dating with dread.

There are a number of aspects of dating that might cause you to feel anxiety:

- *Because you can't control it:* As we saw earlier, because each date and each new person is a new experience, you probably feel out of control; and you are. There is no way to control what will happen, or how the other person will act or respond. However, knowing that you can control your own actions and responses, and having information and techniques for successful dating will put you in control of what really counts -- yourself.

- *Because you don't know how it will end:* Dating has no guarantee of a happy ending. In fact, that's what you're dating for; to check out a new person, and find out whether a partnership will work between the two of you. Not knowing how it will end, along with being worried about rejection and hurt, can really increase your anxiety. Keep in mind that the unknown ending could be a happy one. Be careful not to focus on only the negative possible outcome. Being informed and having steps to follow and learning new techniques will maximize your chances of having a happy outcome, and teach you how to have a good time even with the people who won't be around long.

- *Because it ended before:* Prior pain is often a reason why people dread a new experience. If the last relationship was painful, hurtful and a disaster, it's natural not to want to try it again. "When one door of happiness closes," said Helen Keller, "another one opens. But often we look so long at the closed door that we do not see the one that has opened for us." Reading this guide, and paying attention to the suggestions here will give you a new way to date, one in which the possibility of pain is minimized and the fun is maximized. The past unsuccessful experiences become steps on the way to having a great relationship.

- *Because it will change who you are:* Yes, dating will change who you are, because it's going to cause you to grow emotionally, and most of us don't relish change. "Most of us are comfortable in the environments we have created," writes psychiatrist and author Martin Groder, in *All about Change* "We identify with our sets of habits, attitudes and activities. As a result, it's threatening to our sense of self to pursue habits, attitudes and activities that are unfamiliar... change creates the anxiety of *ambiguity* -- an uncomfortable feeling that causes us to feel as if we don't know exactly who we are." If you keep in mind, however, that the new you will be happier, more socially confident, and very likely in love, you can overcome the dread and get enthused.

Finding love today doesn't have to be dreadful. By following the suggestions here, you can create your own dating style, which is much more practical and realistic for who you are. Part of this process will be to discover what can make it fun for you, and learning how to implement that information; so it will be different from your prior dating and relationship experiences: more adult, and more comfortable. You will actually be able to relax, and have a good time.

The Thrill of It All
Once you have examined and dealt with all the fears, negative expectations and dread that come up when you consider dating, you can get on with the planning and the process.

Being afraid is natural, and a healthy response to facing a situation you've had trouble with before. Your fears are saying, in effect "I've had a bad time with this before; I don't feel prepared to do it again." Respect that message and get prepared and informed. The more competent you feel, the less fearful and more enthusiastic you will feel. You are about to face a lot of new experiences, have a great deal of fun and learn a number of new ways to date. Careful planning will eliminate most of the problems you fear before they even come up. The whole point of this guide is to give you the information and techniques you need to make this an enjoyable and successful process.

Dr. Romance™'s objective in this guide is to give you enough information and help that you can feel confident; because when you are secure and confident, you will also begin to get enthused, excited and ready to have a good time. So go ahead, dig in to these pages, and absorb the information. You'll find that the steps are presented clearly and simply enough that you will feel encouraged and intrigued. Armed with this information, you can let yourself be interested, excited, enthused and even giddy about dating.

CHAPTER TWO

What's in Your Way?

If we were to believe the movies, finding love is either a cinch:

- the person of your dreams walks in, you're instantly intrigued, you flirt expertly while the steam and the background music rise, and you're off to a beautiful, romantic, sexy beginning;
- or a disaster, as in the *Finding Mr. Goodbar* girl-meets- killer or *Fatal Attraction* boy-meets-lunatic scenarios.

Real-life dating actually falls in the enormous middle ground between these two fantasies. It's not a snap, it takes some work, but, with some inside information, it can be done right, and it can lead to lots of fun times and relationship success. What makes the difference is understanding what the potential problems are, and knowing the skills to overcome those problems when they arise.

The Quibbles and the Waffles

If you were a movie character, you'd be sure of yourself, clear on what you want, beautifully turned out, and ready to go. But, you're you: a human being, with some confusion, some doubts and some insecurity, like all the rest of us. When you sincerely prepare to date again, and think about what to do first, you're probably going to have some quibbles: things you give yourself a hard time about;

and some waffles: things you can't decide about. The most common fall into seven categories:

1. *I'm Not Ready*

   These are all the reasons you cook up about not being ready to begin searching for love:

   - I'm not emotionally healed from my last experience
   - I haven't a thing to wear!
   - I don't know how to: talk, flirt, behave, stay safe
   - I have to: lose some weight, grow some hair, get a nose job, get my PhD...
   - I don't have any time

   All of these quibbles are excuses for not getting started, not good, solid reasons. If you are still hurting from your last experience, you may want to attend therapy, but you can still go out and begin meeting new people. Dating again, as I present it here, is not an instant process, and going through the process can be part of your healing process.

   While looking your best is indeed an important part of dating, excuses about clothing, weight, hair and other aspects of your appearance are not a reason to postpone getting out there. Actually, getting your appearance together is one of the first steps toward finding love today.

   If you are insecure about proper behavior, flirting, or just talking to new people; learning how to do that, too, is an excellent beginning.

   If your schedule is so busy that you cannot manage an evening a week, or some weekend time during which to date, you have some organizing to do in your life to be prepared to have a relationship. As you'll see, meeting new people and getting to know them can be integrated into things you already do, and you can organize your life so you'll have enough spare time.

Do research before you go out looking for places to meet people, just as you would in shopping for a new computer or appliance; ask your friends for recommendations, call for information, look in local newspapers for resources, so you know where you want to go, the hours, the open days, what to wear, and what's likely to happen before you waste time acting on wrong assumptions.

2. *No One Will Like Me / I'm Ugly*
    This is related to your quibbles about appearance, but it goes much deeper. If you find that what's stopping you from dating is your own insecurities and lack of self-worth: feeling so bad about yourself that you can't imagine anyone else would like you, getting help is vital. Group or individual therapy, a twelve-step program, or self-esteem classes will help you confront and overcome your inner struggle with yourself. Searching for "self-esteem" or "self-image" in a search engine like Google will bring up many podcasts, books, blogs and classes that can help you sort out your image problems. *It Ends with You: Grow Up and Out of Dysfunction* is my book to help you heal.

    All of these quibbles are clues to the aspects of dating for which you feel unprepared, and by paying attention to your insecurities, you can discover what information and skills you need. Preparing by learning these things is the beginning of your success at the dating process.

3. *It's Going to Be a Disaster Right from the Start*
    Some of your ills you have cured/
    And the sharpest, at least you've survived.
    But what torments of Hell you've endured/
    From evils that never arrived. -Goethe (1749-1832)

    Scaring oneself is not new. Even two thousand years ago the German poet Goethe knew about self-generated fear. It's easy to frighten yourself with negative predictions and "what ifs;" your anxieties projected into the future. Finding love today is a risk, and bound to produce some anxiousness, but it doesn't help to dwell on what could go wrong and scare yourself even more. Instead, focus on what you will do if any of your scary future scenarios come true. For example, If your dire prediction is "I'm going to go to this party, no one will talk to me, and I'll be miserable all night." Neutralize the fear by figuring out what to do if the worst happens. "If no one talks to me, I'll ask the hostess to introduce me to someone, or if I can help pour drinks, to keep myself busy."

If you discourage yourself before you begin, you can make new adventures truly difficult; even if the problems never happen. If you know you can handle whatever comes up, you can have fun even when you don't meet the love of your life on a particular occasion.

4. *Just Like the Last Time*

This quibble comes up if you've had a difficult time in a previous relationship, or a divorce, or sometimes even if a partner has passed away. It's the fear that whatever hurt you before is bound to happen again. It's not surprising, if you were hurt before, that you would be wary of going through it all over again, but it's also not necessary. Treat this quibble like the others in this section: as a signal that you need to know more about the subject. In the case of broken relationships, understanding what went wrong in the first place will go a long way toward assuaging your fears. For example, if you were shocked and surprised by a partner who lied, cheated, or who just announced one day that the relationship was over, perhaps you need to learn more about creating open communication, and choosing people who will be honest with you. When you know you can do something to reduce the odds of a previous problem reoccurring, you will feel more secure.

5. *Love Doesn't Work Anyway*
    You tell yourself love doesn't work for anyone, at any time, so you won't feel bad if it doesn't work for you. Negative attitudes like this one just increase the odds that you'll be miserable and even more nervous, and therefore, make mistakes. Look around you. We live in a time of relationship turmoil, when every couple seems to break up almost before they get started; but, if you look, you'll find that there are lots of couples who are doing fine. They look happy.

    Look for these success stories and focus on them, and you'll feel more encouraged and motivated to pursue finding love of your own. Love can work, if you choose the right partner, and you know the skills. And when it does, it's great!! Even if you don't find the love of your life right away, successful dating is an enjoyable way to fill your time while you're looking.

6. *I Don't Need this/ I'd Rather Be Alone*
    Yeah, sure. You'd rather sit home and eat pizza for one while watching old re-runs. Don't kid around, this is your life you're talking about. Besides, you probably don't feel this way all the time, you waffle back and forth about it. One minute, meeting others looks like a good idea, the next you want to be alone. While you may, indeed, be a person who prefers solitude, and likes living alone, you still need social contacts and friends; and that's what dating is all about. Savvy dating is making good connections with desirable people; and all of us can use as much of that as we can get. You can learn to balance your social life with your privacy, so you get enough of each one.

7. *I Can't Do this to the Kids/ the Cat/ My Roommate/ My Ex/ Myself*

   This may be the ultimate in quibbles. There is bound to be someone in your life you can use to hold you back. This is believing if you go out and meet new people, the people already in your life will suffer. If you think of what you're doing as just making friends until something clicks with someone, you'll have a hard time making this quibble stick. How would meeting new people be a problem for your kids, your cat, your roommate, your ex, or anyone already in your life? Repeat after me: I am not interested in *replacing* anyone already in my life; I do not intend to neglect them or to ignore them. I am simply looking for some new people with whom I can have fun. Keeping your mind firmly planted on that will make sure you don't cause problems in the relationships you already have.

How Will It End?

We all want a happy ending, and we want to know it in advance: like reading the last page of a novel when the story gets scary, to see if it comes out all right. But, dating, like the rest of life, doesn't work that way. You won't know the end until you get there. By following the advice and guidelines given here, however, you can make sure you have good results. And, after all, *you* get to decide when you reach the ending; if you don't give up, you can meet your goals.

Wanting a Guarantee: I Won't Start If I Don't Know How It Ends
The best way to guarantee you won't have a happy ending is to avoid, procrastinate, and put off getting out there. Unless you have a real, working crystal ball, you'll have to take events as they come along. Remind yourself that this is about having a good time; if you take your time, and do it in a logical fashion, there's not too much that can go wrong. You'll meet some nice people, and some strange ones. You'll have some great times, and some not-so-great times. There's no guarantee that you'll meet prince or princess charming

and live happily ever after. But, by following the sensible suggestions laid out for you in this book, you can guarantee that you will meet good people, have a great time, and thoroughly enjoy finding love today.

Worst Case, You'll Live

No matter how badly your experiment goes, if you make sensible choices and take some simple precautions, you'll be safe. The worst thing that will happen is occasional disappointment, a boring evening, being interested in someone who doesn't return the interest, or some other minor problem. The whole point of this book is to help you avoid more serious problems, and greatly increase the odds of having fun and being successful. Yes, people do get emotionally and even physically hurt while dating, we hear the stories in the news all the time. But, we are not always told the circumstances of these horror stories, or how rare they are. Many of the problems are caused by drinking too much, getting intimately involved too fast, and other lapses of judgement. Following the cautions and guidelines set forth here will help you avoid the problems, and maximize your chances of success.

How Long Will It Take?

No one knows how long it will take. The sooner you get started, the better. If you're having a good time in what you're doing, making new friends, and enjoying yourself, it will be fun no matter how long it does take. And speaking of how long it will take, what goal do you have in mind? If you use these recommended guidelines, you'll be connecting with people within a few weeks, and not long after that, you'll find someone to date. If your goal is to find your one true love, your mate for life, that will take a bit longer.

Don't Rush it; it's Going to Take a While

Most of the horror stories you have heard about dating occur when you rush the process. Getting intimately involved with someone you don't know, allowing strangers into your home, or being all alone with someone you just met is just asking for trouble.

Dating successfully is an organized process that will take a little time. You'll begin with carefully looking for the right people in the right places. How you feel about yourself and your own life; and being interested, interesting and happy means a lot more than how rich or handsome you are. Physical looks and outer attributes fade in importance very quickly: your personality and character are what a true partner values.

How Much Will It Hurt?
Despite all precautions, you can still get hurt. Even when you are careful, you can still be disappointed, frustrated, hurt and upset. Life is full of such frustrations and disappointments, but the ones connected to dating can be the most painful, because they involve your self-esteem and your emotional well-being. Dating can be stressful because it involves a lot of new and unknown circumstances. Your whole goal is meeting new people: which often involves trying new activities in new settings. Anything unfamiliar is stressful, because it involves a lot of on-the-spot decision making. When you're in a situation you're not familiar with, you tend to be alert, a bit anxious, and to use more energy than normal. You are trying to size up new people and situations, and thinking about every word you say. All of this is tiring, so, in order to keep dating for enough time to be successful at finding a partner, and to avoid burnout, you will need to learn to pace yourself.

The Rhythm of Dating: Take Occasional Breaks
To pace yourself, learn to follow your energy: pursue a lot of new adventures when you feel energized and enthused, but don't worry if you feel more reclusive from time to time. If you take regular breaks from getting out there, you'll actually be able to do more than if you keep pushing. To give yourself a break from the unfamiliar territory of dating, spend time with good friends or family members, doing familiar things, or retreat totally: stay home

and pamper yourself with favorite foods, music and a well-known movie or book. You'll be surprised how refreshed and re-energized you feel. A change of environment can be energizing or refreshing. If you're in a rut, dating will be exciting and new. If you're tired, stressed, or over-stimulated with new experiences, retreating to familiar friends and surroundings will be restful and restorative.

Your Support System

As with any change you want to make, having a support system will help keep you focused and enthused. Let your best friends and closest family members know what you're doing and enlist them to be your support team.

- *Single Support:* Single friends can go out on some of your new adventures with you; for example, if you want to take a class, you and a friend can go together. Or, enlist a friend to accompany you to the first meeting of a non-profit group you want to join.

- *Emotional Support:* Your support team can also be there to comfort and commiserate with you when you're rejected or hurt, and to remind you how much they all care (especially when Prince or Princess Charming turns out to be a troll). When you're successful, they can cheer you on. You'll get a lot of energy and motivation from sharing your ups and downs with sympathetic caring people.

- *Advice:* There's no expert better than a friend who's been there, done that. If your support team includes people who successfully dated after losing a relationship, don't hesitate to ask for their experience. Their experience can be helpful even though they differ from you, and have different needs, and what worked for them may not work for you. Their ideas can spark more fitting ones of your own. Just as a parent who's been through it all and lived to tell about it can give reassurance and advice to a nervous first-time parent, so your friend with more recent dating experience can be equally helpful and reassuring to you. It's great to hear, "Oh, don't worry about that; I went through that a bunch of times before I got it right." It's both comforting and supportive to hear someone who succeeded tell you you're doing OK.

Make sure your experienced friends have the right kind of experience. Seek out friends who have succeeded in dating the way you want to; not the ones who have created disasters for themselves. Just as you wouldn't ask someone with a DUI for driving lessons, don't ask a relationship disaster expert for advice.

You Goofed? So What? It's an Experiment
You're going to make some mistakes. This is new territory, by definition, and you are not an expert, but an experimenter. Keep that fact firmly in mind, and don't sweat the small stuff. A mistake is very small stuff; it simply gives you a chance for a re-take. Correcting a mistake can lead to better results than if you do it right the first time. Everyone admires you when you can take responsibility for whatever you did wrong, or neglected to do right. "I'm sorry, I know I should have called sooner, but it took me a while to get the nerve up," is far more endearing and impressive than a lot of denial and excuses. It's also an opportunity to continue the relationship, while giving up in self-disgust or self-criticism ends it. The third thing it does is to let the other person know that you are capable of admitting an error and working out a mutual solution; which is not a bad quality for a potential romance to have.

If the mistake is more serious, like drinking too much and driving, or really hurting someone's feelings or insulting them (intentionally or unintentionally), or getting caught in some kind of lie, then the re-take you need is between you and you. Your behavior, and perhaps your thinking process, needs adjustment. If you can't make the adjustment by yourself, call on your support team for help or referrals to experts.

When Someone from Your Past Returns

So, you finally got up the courage to begin finding love. Perhaps you've even met someone you are interested in. That's exactly when a bad penny from your past is likely to turn up. It may be tempting, to go back to the old, familiar person and skip this experimenting thing, but while your chances of working it out with your ex are not absolutely zero, they're not great.

Here are some warning signs that make a second try not likely to succeed:

- You remember only the good, not the bad, history
- Your ex makes promises, but shows no real sign of change
- You still cannot communicate about what went wrong
- You see this as a way to avoid making your own changes
- Things between you start to get sexual immediately
- You're ignoring feelings of doubt and distrust

If you split up before because you had difficulties you couldn't resolve, or if you were dumped by this other person before, what makes you think you can do it again this time, only better? Don't let a returning ex fill you full of nostalgia and lure you back into the same old thing that didn't work last time.

At the very least, if you're considering a re-try, make sure some real change has happened since you last dated your ex. Think long and hard about what went wrong before, and try to make sure you're not repeating the same dynamics. Look for real, hard-won change in your ex, a change of some longstanding duration, not just the ex's declaration that s/he has seen the light, and is ready to come back now. If your ex hasn't changed significantly, the relationship won't change much either. If you truly think that you didn't give the relationship a chance, you might want to try again, but be warned: the odds are not on your side.

You and your ex may want to be friends, which can work if enough time has passed, and if the problems between you were not too bad.

Of course, if you share the parenting of children, it is essential that you find a way to get along.

If you do decide to try renewing the relationship, be certain you discuss your past issues and make some agreements about how this time will be different. If you decide to avoid dating by renewing an old relationship, I highly recommend couple counseling to help you be sure you're really solving the old problems, and not repeating history. There are guidelines for being friends with your ex later in this chapter.

Dating as an Adult Means You Have a History, Not a Blank Slate

Unlike the teenager dating for the first time, you have experience, which will be valuable if you know how to draw on it. But, if your past experience overwhelms you and prevents you from doing what you want to do, it becomes a problem. To date successfully, you need to acknowledge your history, positive and negative, and use the experience you have gained to help you know what to do today.

Memories Can Help or Hurt

Dating will bring up both painful and happy memories of your past, which can also be useful. Noticing and analyzing memories when they come up rather than trying to ignore them, will give you a lot of information. Even a relationship that did not work out can teach you good things. If you list and compare the qualities of each of your past relationship experiences, you can create a composite of desirable qualities you would like to find in the next situation, and the undesirable qualities to watch out for.

You Thought Your Mourning Was Over?

One of the things that happens when a relationship ends is that the hopes and dreams you had for that relationship die with it. No matter how bad the relationship is, as long as it lasts, there's a possibility that things will change and your hopes and dreams be realized. When the relationship finally ends, even if you're relieved, you may be confused to find yourself grieving for the lost possibilities. This can be quite disconcerting, especially if the relationship was very difficult, because your emotional reaction doesn't seem to match your experience. If, in addition to losing these hopes and dreams, you have also lost a partner whom you still loved and still felt attached to: whether your partner died or just left you; you'll also be grieving for that.

To handle your grief properly, you'll need support. Family and friends may be able to give you the support you need, but often that support is not enough, or it fades before you have finished grieving. Individual therapy and grief groups offer more expert and lasting support: you can express as much grief as you need, and your therapist or group will help you resolve it, rather than saying you should be over it by now.

If the current source of grief connects into a more complex issue, such as childhood abandonment, your emotions will be powerful and possibly frightening to your family, friends and yourself. A therapist or facilitated grief group will be more equipped to help you express and resolve these feelings without reacting negatively.

Even after completing grief therapy, however, you won't be completely grief-free. If you have a difficult evening out, or a disappointing encounter, you may find your grief suddenly re-emerging. Also, doing things that remind you of a past relationship, a missing parent, child or sibling, can flood you with grief at unexpected moments, in the middle of your fun. For example, if you lost a spouse with whom you often went skiing, and you go on a skiing trip with some single friends, in the midst of the fun and laughter, you may find yourself feeling very sad. This is entirely normal, especially after the loss of a person you've been close to for a long time.

All you need to do when memories arise in the middle of having fun is take a moment to yourself, and acknowledge your grief. If you allow yourself to feel the sadness and loss, it will pass rather quickly, and you can get back into the event and go on with the day. If you have trouble getting alone, consider going to the bathroom for a few minutes. There's almost always a bathroom available; it's a place you can easily retreat to and be alone.

Social Expectations and Myths: Becoming Myth Free.

A lot of the problems that come up in dating are generated by *social expectations* (how other people think you should behave or things should happen) and *myths* (common beliefs which are not based on fact). Having such expectations and myths can shape your behavior and reactions in ways that create dating problems. Here we will examine the most prevalent of these myths.

There's not enough to Go Around
Our fears often cause us to imagine the worst possible problems, and often media comes up with pseudo-facts that corroborate those fears, as in the news article that temporarily electrified the country (especially women) by stating that there were not enough marriageable men to go around. The statistics showed in the article were later disputed, but the myth persists, because it corroborates our fears. Dating, especially when it's been a while, can bring up worries about your age, your looks, your intelligence, the availability of partners, your safety and other concerns. When such worries bother you, you can always find someone to agree with you that they are real. Unfortunately, your worries can discourage you, and prevent you from thinking clearly and following your plan to date successfully. By ending your worries, you will keep your energy and enthusiasm up.

The Worrier's Guidelines
If you are worrying about any of these potential shortcomings or failures, or nervous about future events and problems, the

following steps will help you overcome the worries and keep your spirits up:

Step 1. If you're feeling anxious or worried, or you can't stop thinking about some event that hasn't happened yet, take a few moments to write down whatever is worrying you. If it's not convenient to write it down, think it through carefully until you can clearly say what you're worrying about. Pinning the worries down and making them clear will stop the overwhelming sensation of vague, unresolvable anxiety.

Step 2. Look at the first item on your list. Ask yourself "Is there anything I can do about it now?" If you're at work, and worrying about a dating issue, or if you're worried about what to wear to an event which won't occur until next week or next year, there may not be anything you can do right now. Or, you may realize you can call someone for information or support, jot down some ideas, or make a reminder note.

Step 3. If there is something you can do, do it. Don't use worry as a way to procrastinate, or as a mental notepad: as in "I'm worried that I'll forget something when I shop for food for the potluck tomorrow."

If you're worried about...

- ... An event that will happen tomorrow or next week, and you can make a list of things you need to do, or items to get, or people to call, go ahead and do it.
- ... Your dirty laundry, use the time to do the laundry.
- ... Sexual safety, see the advice later in this chapter, look it up on the Internet, or call your doctor, or call a sex hotline and ask some questions.
- ... Cooking dinner for a date (but you're at work) write out the menu or list of ingredients. If you're at home, get out a cookbook and plan the meal.
- ... How to dress for a party, call a friend for advice and lay out your clothes, clean and ready, in advance.

42

Step 4. When you've done what you can, or made your lists or notes, then distract yourself: get busy doing something else, or read, or take a walk or a bath. Repeat the above steps every time you catch yourself worrying.

You're a Special Person; You Only Need One Other
One thing we have a tendency to worry about is whether there are enough suitable people out there. No matter how much you hear about how few eligible men or women there are for your age range, or that all the appropriate ones are already taken, take heart. You are an individual unlike any other, and you have an advantage if you are following the successful process outlined here. Out of all the people in your town or city, you only need one, and if you do what is suggested here, go to the appropriate places where you can meet suitable people, as outlined in the following chapters, your chances of meeting a suitable partner are excellent, and making new friends is a sure thing.

If Your Family Didn't Love You, Someone Else Still Can

If your family history was difficult, and you don't know what healthy relationships are, you can feel that you're doomed; and relationships will never work for you. While you may need to do some extra work to correct the damage, you can still enjoy the dating experience, make some friends and even find a suitable relationship.

If you grew up in a problem family, you may worry that you don't know what normal family interaction looks like. If there was an alcoholic, a depressed parent, a volatile or violent relationship, a missing parent, or even a foster situation, you may not have witnessed enough normal discussion, decision-making, problem-solving and affection to know how to do it in your own relationship.

Relationship difficulties caused by your lack of healthy role models might be one reason you are dating now. If your past relationship repeated your early family problems, you may fear you'll never be able to love or be loved.

By following the steps set forth in the next chapter, you can avoid repeating those old patterns. Keep focused on your goal of meeting someone with whom you can create a loving relationship. If your problem is difficult, learning to date successfully could cause you to seek counseling or therapy. If so, good for you. You'll learn what you need to know to date again successfully.

You've Beat Bad Odds Before, this Is No Problem
If you're worried that the odds are against you, and that you won't succeed because few people do, you need to re-direct your thinking. Remember: you have been through difficulties before, you have learned new things before, you will survive this, and it will be worth it.

Each of your life experiences has taught you something, which means you know more that you did the last time. You are following expert advice, which will increase your chances of success. The fact that you're reading this book shows that you care about the result, you're thinking carefully, and you want to approach dating from an organized, informed point of view, which will make you more effective and successful.

In my experience as a relationship counselor, I find that people who look for a relationship after losing one; if they do it thoughtfully and with a plan, almost always find someone who suits them better than the last person, because they've grown in wisdom and learned from experience.

You Can't Lose When You Make Friends
The best way to guarantee a good outcome in this process is to seek to make friends. If you set a goal to meet new friends and have good times, you'll succeed. When you approach your search as a

search for friends, you can relax the stringent requirements you would have for a lover or partner, and notice everyone: because anyone could turn out to be a good friend. When you relax and open up your criteria in this way, you will be open to meeting more of the people you encounter, and to finding out about them. Who knows, one of them may have a sibling or a friend who could turn out to be your soul mate.

Remember the old saying: "birds of a feather flock together". In this context, that means if you find good quality people you enjoy, and become friends, you will meet their other friends; who will be similar quality people. Most of the people you meet and like will know other people who are quite similar. Thus, every new friend can bring a network of new people, as desirable as the original friend, into your life.

Do You Only Get to Love One Person in a Lifetime?
In this day of a 50% divorce rate, it's getting harder to believe there can only be one person in the world for you, but the myth still persists. There are lots of songs, poems, and movies about the one true love you can't survive without.

No One Will Match Your Last, but They'll Be Nicely Different
Anyone who has loved someone for a long time and then lost them naturally feels that there's no way they can be replaced. Of course, no one who is dear to you and now gone can exactly be replaced. There are many ways to love people, and a number of people you can love. Just as you can love various members of your family differently, and just as you can care deeply about several dear friends, in different ways, so you can also find more than one person who are compatible enough to fall in love with and create a workable relationship. If you were very much in love with a prior partner, you may be surprised to find that a new person has attributes and qualities you really enjoy; things you never knew were missing before.

It's fortunate that we are able to love more than one person, because it's so easy to be attracted to someone with big relationship issues. The point of this search is to find several people who are appealing to you, so you can sort through their character traits and foibles, until you find someone who is not only attractive, but also healthy for you. For this reason, later in this guide, you'll find out how to choose a relationship from the neck up as well as from the neck down: that is, using your judgement as well as your sense of chemistry and attraction.

"If I, after four wretched marriages and a whole lifetime of fucking up people's lives, and having them fuck up my life, could arrive at a marriage as happy and terrific as I've got, *anybody* can do it... If *I* can be happy, anybody in this universe can be happy. " -science fiction writer Harlan Ellison

At the turn of the 20th century, when social mores were more restrictive, and people didn't move around as much as they do today, meeting a new partner was more difficult. Today, we have more personal freedom, and neither gender has to wait for the other to make a move, or for a proper introduction. Everyone has more mobility and unlimited opportunities to connect, and a bigger population and more social outlets makes meeting new people a lot easier. The big question is not "Are there enough eligible people I can meet?" but "How, out of all these people, do I choose the one with whom I can really be successful?"

I'm Too Old to Date
You can hear the age myth stated by people from 25 years old to advanced senior citizens. I personally know of three ladies who met suitable gentlemen and got married at the ages of 78, 85 and 87. It's never too late to meet a mate.

Seniors in Love Anecdotes (names are changed)
- *Rose* was taking a world cruise. She would be on the ship for over three months of luxury and adventure. At 87, she had

been widowed for many years, and her children were not only grown, but middle-aged. She was still active and healthy, and she wanted to take this cruise while she was still able to do it. One day, the cruise held a party for all the singles on board, and Rose decided to go; perhaps she'd meet some new friends. As people were introduced, she was astounded to hear a man's name which recalled her past. She went up to him, and introduced herself. It was true! Robert was the very man she had dated as a young woman. Things had not worked out when they were younger, but this time they were not going to lose each other. After getting reacquainted on the ship, they were married six months later.

- *Claire* had spent her entire life in obedience to her parents. She stayed home after her father died, to care for her elderly mother, who eventually became demented and difficult. Claire even ran the local post office in the small village she lived in, because she could do that from her home. She almost never went out. When her mother finally died, Claire was 60 years old, and the federal government closed her small post office, and transferred her to a post office job at the county seat. There she met George, another postal worker, and her contemporary. They began having lunches together, and developed a friendship. After a number of years, they both retired and continued their relationship. At age 78, Clara became a bride for the first time in her life, and the ladies of her small town threw her a wedding shower. Seeing her opening gifts, and holding up lovely, lacy lingerie was truly the picture of a dream come true.

- *Vera*, 85 years old, had been married to a military officer, and lived all over the world. She and her husband raised several children, and had many grandchildren and even great - grandchildren. Her husband had died a few years ago, and she had moved to California to be close to her younger sister, who was also now widowed. The sisters lived close together, and traveled often together. One day, the phone rang, and when Vera picked it up, a voice on the other end said "do you remember me?" It was Ed, whom Vera had been engaged to when she was 18. He had tracked her down through people who knew her in their old home town. They hadn't married because Vera had discovered that Ed had a drinking problem. He had long since become sober, married, and raised a family of his own, but his wife had died a few years before. Vera decided to go to the nearby city where Ed lived, just for a couple of days, to meet him and talk. Her sister got a call. She was not coming home right away. In fact, she didn't come home for two weeks. She and Ed were married six months later.

If you ask your friends, co-workers and family members, you'll hear many more stories of people who met and fell in love at advanced ages. It's obvious from these stories that age does not have to hold you back from meeting someone to love. There is nothing about you that will stop you from meeting people except your own fear or reluctance. When you're a teenager, an age difference of 10 or more years makes a vast difference in your experience and your outlook on life. Such a difference can interfere with communication, life goals, outlook, and relationship experience. In addition, the social reaction to such a relationship is often very negative. If one partner is underage, a sexual relationship is even against the law. But, as we get older, life experience and emotional growth even things out. A ten-year or more difference in your ages makes little difference in how well you can conduct your relationship. Don't focus on an arbitrary difference in your ages. If you are getting along, you have good communication and problem-solving, and you love each other, that's a precious thing, and far more important than any age difference could be. If other people have a problem with it, let it be their problem.

All Men/women Are… (Violent, Users, Smarter, Crazy, More Handsome)

Many myths are based on a negative view of life and love, often because the people who promote them had negative experiences themselves. As we have discussed before, difficult family or relationship experiences can affect your view of relationships and the possibility of being loved.

This is why I stress:

- finding quality people to date
- looking in appropriate places
- taking your time before getting emotionally involved
- interviewing new dates, and paying attention to the information you get
- using your friends network for support, and
- checking up on the people you meet.

Anyone can meet a person who is a problem. They don't wear signs. It's not your fault if you meet someone who doesn't have his or her act together. However, if you stick around someone who obviously can't function well enough to be a good partner, you can fix that problem; learn to let go of bad apples. Difficult people aren't usually a problem if you keep them at a distance. They're a giant problem if you let them into your life. This guide will give you many ways to protect yourself from such problems.

You're Looking for a Person, Not a Category
You can be led astray if you are too concerned about categories such as wealth, education, good family, impressive career, fancy car, and designer clothes, or even ethnicity or religious background. To find a quality person with whom to share your life, you must look beyond those surface clues, and deeper into the person. Con artists of all types know very well how to exploit appearances to lure you in and take advantage of you. If you follow the guidelines which are fully explained in the succeeding chapters, you will not be vulnerable to people who want to take advantage of you. Scaring yourself about Molesters, Rapists, Alcoholics, Narcissists, and other kinds of dangerous types is just

another needless worry. Each person you meet presents an opportunity for you to find out who he or she is, and if you use the general precautions set forth in this book, you'll be in more danger of being struck by lightning than of being harmed by a potential date. There are more good people than bad people out there, and with a little know-how, and proper caution, it's pretty easy to recognize the difference.

Every Person Is Different
To get to know a new person, and be known, takes a little time, because each of us is unique. People don't fit into neat, tidy classifications. You can observe someone and think "Oh, she has good manners, she must be classy." and then find out she has a problem with rage, overspending or alcohol. On the other hand, some perfect gems come in rough clothing. Many clients who are in good relationships with wonderful partners have told me "I wouldn't have looked twice at him if we hadn't gotten to know each other first." Or, "She wasn't "my type", but after I saw her in action volunteering in the political campaign, I realized she was an extraordinary person, with great ethics, and very caring." A popular one today is "If we had met in person, before we exchanged emails and phone calls for a while, I probably wouldn't have realized what a good guy he is." Each person you meet along the path has unique personality traits, desirable and undesirable. Giving yourself the time to get to know them enables you to sort them out.

You Don't Have to Repeat Your History
No matter how bad your history has been, you don't have to re-create it. You can learn to interact in different ways, and to correct problems that come up. This guide is about correctly and successfully making new connections. If you feel out of control and unable to follow the guidelines here, you may need to work with a counselor to make the necessary changes, just as you might work with a personal trainer to correct and improve your workouts, or a

nutritionist to evaluate and correct your diet, or even take computer classes to figure out how to do what you want to do. If your early background was dysfunctional and toxic, or your previous partners have been abusive or addictive, you may need to be suspicious of your first choices. That is, because of your early experience, you may be conditioned to be attracted to a particular character flaw. That is, the people you automatically are drawn to, and feel comfortable with initially, may be exactly the people you should stay away from. In such cases, familiarity is a trap. If you know this about yourself, and can resist the pull of the dysfunction, you can meet other, better people to date. If you have trouble changing this focus, counseling can help.

We're all in the Same Boat

Everyone who faces meeting new people as an adult has similar worries and insecurities. It's that return of adolescent feelings I discussed in the last chapter.

You Are Not Alone in Feeling…

- Vulnerable
- Like a Loser
- Afraid of Rejection
- Awkward, Unacceptable

Everyone feels equally insecure about connecting today. Some hide it better than others, some have been at it longer, and have become less nervous, but everyone has been through it. If you present a friendly, pleasant demeanor and you are open to getting to know people, they will be relieved and pleased. Here is the perfect place to practice the Golden Rule: treat others exactly as you would like to be treated, and you will have plenty of good responses. Each new situation will produce the above list of qualms, but keep in mind you're there to make friends. Find the safest-looking person in the room, and chat with them. You'll feel better, and then you can move on to greeting others. After a few minutes of pleasant conversation with new acquaintances, you will relax, and your anxieties will be forgotten.

Sexual Silliness and Sexual Safety

You only have to look at the current news stories to see how powerful a force sexuality is, and has always been. People in responsible positions, who should know better, are often brought down by lack of sexual self-control. It is no less a danger for you. Here are some brief pointers, which I will discuss in more detail later in the book.

Only Be Sexual When and If You Want to

One of the biggest causes of sexual problems in dating is allowing yourself to be caught up in the moment, persuaded or coerced, or just deluded into having sex when you don't really want to. Most of the time, having sex too soon after meeting someone will derail the possibility of developing a more lasting intimate relationship. This happens for several reasons:

- feeling like intimate strangers is awkward
- either or both of you can feel used
- it gives each of you a negative impression of the other
- the other person may only be interested in sex
- if alcohol was involved, you appear dysfunctional

Although you can have fun while dating, at the core, it is a serious business. If you're really looking for a suitable partner, you need to appear suitable and emotionally healthy as well. Promiscuous sex, especially in today's social atmosphere, does not look healthy. "To dash from one person to another, reveling in the wicked pleasure of infinite possibility is best accomplished it seems to her during youth," says Judith Martin, "Miss Manners is tired of listening to the pathetic tales of those abandoned in middle life by overgrown boys or girls who have only just made that discovery." I am not admonishing you against sex for fun, as long as you practice safer sex. Rather, I am saying don't expect a meaningless sex encounter to develop into a more serious relationship. If you want those encounters, keep them separate from your dating process, and don't confuse the two.

Safety in the Age of STDS: What You Need to Know
We hear a lot about the danger of HIV, AIDS and Chlamydia in the news, but there are more prevalent sexually transmitted diseases (STD's) out there to protect yourself from. You cannot know for sure what the sexual practices and history of a new partner are; no matter how honest they may seem to be, or how much you trust them. People are notoriously uncomfortable disclosing their sexual history, especially if they're concerned that it will damage their relationship with you. This produces the paradox that the more your new date cares about you, the more pressure he or she feels not to tell you the truth about sexual history. Add to this the fact that there are many STD's a person may not realize they have, such as certain forms of Herpes Simplex II virus. Protecting yourself should be automatic at least until the relationship progresses to the stage where both of you wish to be tested (with full knowledge of the other) for all STD's, and remain sexually monogamous after receiving the test results.

A mere listing of the potential diseases, like this one from Tufts University, is sobering:

Sexually Transmitted Diseases

- Syphilis — bacterial infection, treatable and curable in its early stages. Classic symptom is a painless sore, or chancre.
- Gonorrhea — Bacterial infection, not easily detectable — symptoms are painful urination, vaginal or penile discharge. Curable with antibiotics.
- Herpes — viral infection — Chronic, no cure. Can spread silently. Painful genital sores can be controlled with drugs.
- Chlamydia — Bacterial infection — Curable, but chronic if untreated. Symptoms similar to Gonorrhea.

- Genital Warts — Highly contagious, strongly connected with cancer. Very difficult to cure, chemically or surgically. Internal warts may be undetectable.
- HIV — Human Immune Virus — can cause AIDS (Auto Immune Deficiency Syndrome). Transmitted by blood to blood or semen to blood contact. Chronic, recent drugs can control it.

All these diseases can be transmitted by sexual contact, and none of them are pleasant. If you're going to engage in sex with people you don't know well, it's essential that you protect yourself. Here are the most important ways to protect yourself sexually, according to the Tufts University Wellness Newsletter:

Preventing STDs
- Use latex condoms and a spermicide. Condoms and spermicide, in combination, will protect you from most STDs
- Be Observant. Don't have sexual contact with anyone who has genital or anal warts, sores, a visible rash, a discharge or any other odd symptoms.
- Be selective. Know who your partner is.
- Be informed. Recognize symptoms, and get tested. Most AIDS testing facilities also teach about symptoms and prevention of all STDs.
- Be responsible. If you think you've been exposed, don't have sex again until you've seen a doctor, been diagnosed and treated.

Because the scope of this book is limited, this information is condensed and minimal. Your doctor, Planned Parenthood, or local emergency room will have more detailed information.

Sexual Rules and Courtship
Although you may believe that you know what the sexual rules or agreements are, you could be wrong. Clear communication, paying

attention to the signs given by the other person, and taking good care of yourself are essential.

Sexual Contact Does Not a Commitment Make
Being an adult does not protect you from wishful thinking, lack of experience and naive mistakes. Sexual deprivation may make you more vulnerable to passion, and so can alcohol and drugs. The consequences of sex with the wrong person can be serious; don't mistake sweet talk and promises for commitment. As Carole King so memorably sang: "Tonight, the light of love is in your eyes/but will you love me tomorrow?" The consequences of STDs, unwanted pregnancies and broken hearts are painful and can last a lifetime.

Dangerous Liaisons
Not only can STDs be dangerous, but people can, too. As the movies and the news reports have shown, it's not always easy to tell which strangers are dangerous, and which are not. Here are some guidelines for protecting yourself and telling the difference. Wherever you meet your new friends, there are precautions you can take to keep yourself safe.

How to Keep Yourself Safe from Violence
1. *Don't be Alone.* Wherever you meet someone, do not allow yourself to be alone with them too quickly. If you decide you want to pursue the relationship, don't go to the other person's home, or allow him or her in yours. Rather, meet for coffee or lunch in a public place, or go somewhere in a group. Even people you think you know, unless you have met their friends, family and spent considerable time with them, can mislead you about their motives.
2. *Don't Drink.* When you're on a new date, don't drink more than a minimal amount (depending on your size, no more than one or two drinks). Do not ride in the other person's car, or drive him or her in yours.
3. *Resist Ridicule and Pressure.* People who are likely to commit violence, or who are not really interested in a relationship,

are often very resistant to such self-protectiveness, and may ridicule you or pressure you to take a risk, to trust them. The more a prospective date does this, the more careful you need to be. This behavior is a clear message that your new acquaintance doesn't value your feelings or your safety.

4. *Don't Let Your Guard Down Too Soon.* Stalking, date rape, and domestic violence are types of violence that often show up later in a committed relationship. Knowing someone for a few months may not be enough time to tell if you can trust them. I'll cover signs to watch out for in later chapters.

Friends with Benefits

It sounds so easy to have sex with someone you already know: you can bypass the whole 'meeting strangers' thing. However, if you're thinking about having sex with a friend, be very careful, because it is not easy to preserve a friendship once you have sex. You may think you can control your feelings, but it's not so simple.

- If one of you becomes romantically attached as a result of the sex, the friendship will probably not survive.

- If you've done it before, and you know you can keep your feelings in check, you might be successful, but what about your friend? Are you sure he or she is aware of his or her own feelings and motives?

- Think about it in advance and talk about it a lot

- Are you going to keep dating others while you're doing this FWB thing?

- What if one of you falls in love with someone else?

- What if you just want out of the deal after a while?

- What if only one of you falls in love, instead of remaining friends?

Keep talking throughout the FWB arrangement. It sounds a lot more fun and easier than it really is. The benefit is being able to have sex with someone you know, rather than someone new. The disadvantages are: It could be the end of the friendship. One person could fall in love, while the other doesn't want to pursue more of a relationship. It may keep you from finding a real relationship, because you're too comfortable to look. If you start to develop feelings, pay attention! Don't ignore it. Let your partner know, and watch the reaction. If you don't get a positive response, cut off the sex. That's the way to see if the other person is also emotionally attached or not. Don't languish in a friends-with-benefits relationship when you want more. If they suddenly meet someone else and marry, you'll be devastated. If you want to cut off the sex, you need to explain why you're doing it. "I'm developing deeper feelings for you, and since you don't seem to return them, I have to stop having sex with you. I'd like to still be friends." Or, "I can't even be your friend for a while, because I'm grieving."

Maintaining this type of relationship is not easy for anyone. It only seems easy at the beginning. My office is full of people who had their hearts broken this way. Older people tend to be a little wiser and more cautious about it than younger people, but all ages get hurt. Don't just let things develop on their own. Definitely talk about it beforehand, or as soon as possible. You need to establish that the friendship is important to both of you, and you don't want to ruin it. You also need to talk about feelings, to open that subject for future discussion. If you want to turn a friendship into a full-on couple relationship, and you're serious about it, then you need to talk about that, too. Your friendship will be altered forever when you have sex for the first time. You have things to lose here, and things to gain. Make some agreements, discuss the above questions, and keep talking about it.

Back to being friends
Friendships that go from friends to lovers back to friends can be very close, because you know each other so well. The first thing you need to do is talk about it. Make a deal that you won't do anything

that would jeopardize your friendship, and stick to it. (That means, acting as a friend, and not acting jealous if he/she has a date.) The more emotionally mature you are, the easier it is to re-establish the friendship. Openness increases intimacy. So friends who can talk about everything feel closer than friends who can't. However, friendships have more limits on sharing than lover relationships do. If you've found someone new, you have to consider your sexual partner, too, who might not like his or her privacy invaded.

It is possible to re-establish a friendship after the romantic line has been crossed, but it's not always easy. If both of you are in agreement that you were better as friends, re-developing the friendship is easier than if one of you still wants the romance. Surprisingly enough, many people do become friends again after they've divorced or split up. Here are some guidelines for doing that successfully.

Guidelines for Being Friends with Your Ex
If your ex has been hanging around, helping you out with things around the house, eating dinner with you and the kids, or just calling you up to talk about good times in the past. Old, friendly feelings seem to be coming back. Can you really revert to being friends? Here's how to see if you and your ex can make friendship work.

- Go very slowly. It takes time to get re-organized as friends. Talk about your friendship and tell the truth. If it's going to work, it goes better if you go more slowly, and you'll have a chance to build a better foundation than before.

- Treat it like a new friendship. Start from the beginning, and do it differently: you have to figure out the difference between being lovers and being friends.

- Be conscious about being friends: talk about what you miss about your friendship; if you cannot talk honestly about what changed and what to do differently, you won't succeed.

- Make sure your ex wants the friendship as much as you do. If there are unresolved old feelings, you need to talk about them.

- If you run into difficulty, seek therapy to repair the friendship and resolve the past problems in your relationship.

Permanence vs. Freedom

It is not unusual to want permanence and also to crave freedom and wish to avoid hurt. Most of us want that. The best way to find it however, is not through being too pushy or rejecting. The best way to find a potential partner is to find and develop friends, and, from that network of new friends find a special someone. This method increases your chances for permanence and also your chances for safety from hurt. Remember, anyone you meet will have had as much difficulty as you have in finding a good relationship. By working on the dynamics between you, developing teamwork and partnership, you can guarantee enough personal freedom to be comfortable within commitment. If the relationship works well, neither you nor your partner will want to let it get away, and making the commitment will be easy for both of you, because you'll be committing to a proven thing.

No matter how much closeness or personal space you want, you can find a partner who will be able to work out a mutually satisfactory relationship with you. You can also design your dating strategy to suit you and be fun for you to carry out. This entire process begins with you knowing what is important to you, and then systematically setting out to find it for yourself.

Follow the Relationship — Don't Drag it

To find out what kind of a relationship you have, you must follow it; not lead it. Allow the relationship to progress for a while, and then look back to see what kind of relationship is developing. If one of your dates becomes serious enough to be exclusive, then do your very best to make the relationship work smoothly. In this way, you'll maximize your good times with this current partner, and also see what it takes to get along, and whether you would be willing to do it permanently. This does not mean you should give in to everything the other person wants, or not bring up issues which need to be discussed; it simply means don't push for more than your partner wants to give in terms of commitment. Rather, learn from what is being offered.

Once you've taken a good look at what is in your way, you're ready to move forward.

CHAPTER THREE

Ready, Set…..

Okay, Ready, Set... Oh, you don't feel quite ready? Good. That's the first step. Setting up your dating process to be successful right from the first will make the whole thing easier and less anxiety-producing. "The people who are most successful have laid the foundations for their actions well in advance of the moment of challenge." Writes Deng Ming-Dao in *Everyday Tao*

Since you're probably going to be dating for a while, the point is to make it a fun experience, and be successful at the same time. People will be most attracted to you when you are having a great time, and enjoying a lifestyle they would want to join. So, let's set this up to be fun, not only because you'll enjoy it more, but because you'll be more attractive that way.

Be Irresistible: Don't Resist it
The best way to be irresistible to others is to let go of whatever resistance *you* have to them. Don't begin dating focused on what you *don't* want; rather focus on what you're discovering. Even where safety issues are concerned, your focus should be on the desirable, quality people you want to meet, rather than on what you're afraid you'll find. Focus on the kinds of fun times you want to have, not on what awful things you're afraid might happen.

From here on, every decision you make will be based on "is this going to get me closer to my goal?" And what is your goal? To meet new good-quality friends, to have a great time, and to eventually establish a healthy, lasting relationship.

Let it Be a Learning Process
Don't be worried about not knowing what to do. You're a beginner at this, and letting people know that is fine. It's not important that you look like an expert. In fact, if you look like you've been dating forever, you'll be less desirable to most people. "It is better to ask some of the questions than to know all the answers," advised philosopher James Thurber.

Having a beginner's mind (Chapter One) works great here. Accept that everything you're doing now is new to you, and open yourself to learning about it. Wide-eyed wonder at whatever happens is very attractive. I'm not talking about being brainless or thoughtless. On the contrary. A beginner's mind is alert, observing, and open to new ideas. Your objective is to learn: about what people are doing, who they are, what the possibilities are and how it all fits in to your goals.

Everything you've learned about relationships and dating in your past is certainly useful, and you'll draw on it as we go along, but your general approach to this process is as a beginner: "I'm new at this, I want to learn." As a beginner, you can open lots of conversations by simply asking questions about what's going on.

Have Fun with it
Instead of focusing on how nervous you are, look around you for what's going on that you might enjoy. For example, when you're attending an event (a private party, a class, a workshop, a charity or political event) you haven't experienced before, I recommend finding a job to do. Volunteer to greet people and take tickets, or keep the food table replenished, or hand out name tags. It will give you a feeling of belonging, a great excuse to meet everyone, and

you'll be busy enough to keep your nervousness at bay. The hosts (generally the most influential people) will get a great impression of you, and remember you later. As an added bonus, volunteering often gets you a discount on the cost of attending the event.

Rather than focus on dating, choose the kinds of activities you'd enjoy to begin with. Take classes in cooking, sports, dancing, yoga, automotive mechanics, great books or current movies and other activities that appeal to you, join teams, get involved in church, charitable or political activities, participate in hiking, biking or bird watching. The most desirable and emotionally healthy people will be doing these fun and fulfilling things. Events and venues organized for singles are called "meat markets" because they create a deadly mix of desperate people who have nothing in common except loneliness. Don't go there. Stick with activities that are fun, healthy, challenging and stimulating. That way you'll enjoy every event, improve your health or outlook, and make friends, even if you don't meet the person of your dreams this week.

Use a Positive Approach

Motivation comes from appreciation and celebration. That is, if you feel positive about what you are doing and the people you are with, you'll be more motivated to continue. It won't be necessary to force yourself to attend things that feel great, and you'll be a lot less anxious.

Steps to Enhance Your Experience

To enhance your positive experience, do the following steps before every new activity:

1. Make a mental note of the possibilities: Can you learn something there? Can you meet a new friend? Will just getting out of the house and around new people feel good?
2. Remind yourself of your goals: You're there to meet friends, to have fun, to eventually make a connection.
3. Review your positive personal qualities: What do your friends like about you? What do you like about you? Your

intelligence, your sense of humor, your style, your conversation skills? Are you a kind and caring person? Reminding yourself of these qualities means you will enter the event radiating that positive energy.

The Tennis Match

Once you are at an event, and meeting people, you need to create the proper energy level to attract people. This does not mean being hyper-active, giddy and over-the-top. Too much energy makes you look anxious. On the other hand, if you appear lethargic and passive, people are not going to be attracted either. Match your energy to the energy of the people at the event. Obviously, if you're dancing or playing sports, the energy level will be pretty high. If you're having quiet conversations at a cocktail party, or on a planning committee, or stuffing envelopes for a charity event, the energy will be more mellow and focused.

Conversations at events you attend should be like tennis matches. That is, the other person serves: he or she asks a question or makes a statement. Then, you volley back: you answer the question with the kind of answer that invites a response. For example:

She: "How do you know our hostess?"

You: "I met her at a class, how do you know her?"

Or: "I met her at class, doesn't she throw a great party?"

This invites your companion to respond, and keeps the volley going. If the conversational thread ends, the next serve is yours. If you have to re-start the conversation too often, excuse yourself and move on. That person is not interested enough. If you force the other person to do all the conversational work, he or she will move on pretty quickly. One-syllable answers are a pretty clear indication of lack of interest, even if you didn't mean it to be that way.

What Are You Projecting/ Receiving?

We all give off lots of information in addition to what we are saying. How we are dressed, posture, fidgeting, where we are looking, facial expressions and general energy all communicate feelings, attitude, status and other information. If you are in your beginner's mind you will be alert to the information coming from the person you are meeting: What impression are you getting? What about the person interests you? Is your response to this person positive or negative?

Be aware also that the other person is picking up a lot of unconscious information from you. This is one reason preparation is so important. If your mental attitude is positive, and you are focused on your goals, and maintaining a beginner's mind, the unintentional signals you are giving are more likely to be inviting. If you are thinking negatively, criticizing yourself, or worrying about what everyone thinks of you, your subconscious energy will be unattractive.

Attitude Counts

As a perfect illustration of this, a TV news magazine did an experiment. They hired an actual, gorgeous model, and one of their staffers who was moderately attractive, slightly overweight, and no match for the model's beauty. Both were dressed tastefully. They took the women to a popular club, and gave them the following instructions. The model was to be unresponsive, give one-syllable answers, and generally appear uninterested and cold. The plainer woman was to be her normal, vivacious self. A hidden camera watched the action.

As you might expect, the gorgeous model got more initial attention. But, within ten minutes, there was a lively, interested group around the non-model, and the model sat alone. It was a graphic depiction of how much more important personality is than looks.

While women and men may be attracted to a stereotypically handsome or gorgeous face and figure, most will be won over by an open, inviting personality pretty quickly. Whether you're male or female, if you're bright, alert, friendly and interested, you will attract plenty of people.

Seek Friends - Not Lovers
By now you know my emphasis on making friends: it's the real key to successful dating. Making friends accomplishes several things:

- New friends make your activities fun
- Seeking friends will make you less anxious
- When you do choose someone to date, it won't be a total stranger.
- It's much safer
- It takes the pressure off you and the other person
- You'll already know your date is interested in you.
- You will have a lot more fun without the performance anxiety

I don't recommend dating strangers. Why waste all that time, money and energy on someone you may not even enjoy? Like it or not, asking for a date is usually interpreted as a statement of intention, and expectations tend to rise. Therefore, wise people date selectively, with forethought. Before going out on a date with someone new, spend some casual time together. Going out for coffee, to lunch, to a group activity, or sharing expenses keeps the expectations and the pressure, lower. Making friends is easy; dating strangers is too hard.

To maximize your fun, reserve special evenings out:
- for people who have established a good reason to get closer
- for lovers who want to spice up their lives with romance or celebrate a special occasion,
- for old friends or family when you want to show them they're special

When you think about it, dating is a terrifying idea! It has become a grueling ritual in which you're supposed to go out with someone you hardly know, usually pay an expensive tab, have a wonderful time, and fall in love forever. Does that sound realistic to you? It doesn't to me, either.

Don't Be Afraid to Try
That's why this process of meeting friends and getting to know people removes the struggle. If you're willing to try, and take a few baby steps, you'll find it's easier than you thought. Check out some activities, some classes, some social events and volunteering opportunities. Try some events at your church if you are connected to one, or try attending a new church if you're not. Sometimes, it only takes a phone call to realize the activity is not for you, sometimes it takes a few visits before you feel comfortable enough. Remember, when you're checking out options, to look for several things:

1. Is the activity something you'll enjoy doing? If you're an outdoor enthusiast, check out local nature and hiking groups. On the West Coast, for example, hikes and camping outings with the Sierra Club are a great way to meet people. You can get to know a person well while hiking a trail, sharing snacks and enjoying the view.
2. Are enough appropriate people there? Are there people of your age range, a good gender balance? Are the people interesting to you? If not, try something else.
3. Have you tried all the options? For example, if you're a senior, and the local Senior Center seems really boring, have you tried it on its busiest afternoon or evening? If your own branch of a particular church denomination or synagogue is mostly the wrong age group, have you checked out the other branches in your town? If you love kids, is there a volunteer option where you can meet others who enjoy helping kids?
4. Have you asked people for a personal recommendation? For example, if you take a cooking class, ask the other students about the local farmers' markets, and perhaps suggest you go together.

Try new things with an open-minded attitude. If you don't like the group or event, you don't have to go again.

You and You: How Do You Feel?
The most central relationship in this process is the one you have with yourself. Keep checking in to see how you feel about what you're doing. Are you going too fast? Too slow? Are you feeling uncomfortable with the place you're visiting right now? What do you think of this person you're talking to? Are you bored? Excited? Getting this kind of feedback from yourself can make a profound difference in your experience. If you frequently evaluate how you're doing, you won't get too far from your main objective. And you'll know when you need to change what you're doing to have a better time.

Set Your Scanner to On
You can improve your experience is by being observant. The first time you go to a new setting, or meet new people, hold back a bit and spend the first half hour or so just observing what's going on. See who knows who, how people behave with each other, and where the action is. By observing people before you meet them, you can determine who you would most like to meet, and perhaps even learn some things about your choice. Staying in touch with your own feelings will keep you safer. In my many years of counseling people who have survived relationship disasters, I find that, looking back, my clients can always recognize the warning signs in their earliest encounters with their ex. Because of their excitement, they ignored what they suspected. Remember, you're here to learn; about other people and about yourself.

Notice the People around You
By observing the people in attendance, you can learn a lot. If you're in a class, watch who seems to be most knowledgeable, who helps others, who tries to impress the teacher, who doesn't care, who needs help. If you're at a party, watch who seems to be genuinely

liked, who clowns around, who is friendly, who is shy. Notice what people are wearing, and anything unusual about them. You can use it to begin a conversation later. What interests you about different people? Remember, too, what you're looking for. In the next chapter, you'll explore what the ideal mate would be for you. Armed with that information, you will be able to observe people to see who seems to have the proper characteristics.

Conversation Is Available Anywhere
You don't have to be at an organized event to practice your conversational skills. Standing in line at the bank or supermarket, waiting at the Laundromat for your clothes to dry, in a shared ride, or sitting at the local coffee club on your lunch hour are all good opportunities to begin a conversation. You'll meet a lot more nice people if you stay off your phone. Good communication saves time. If you are willing to ask a direct question, give an honest answer, speak or hear the truth about where you stand with someone, you can stop beating around the bush or being confused, which wastes your valuable time.

Because you have been observant, you will have plenty of ideas to talk about. If you're in the grocery store, for example, and the person in line in front of you has charcoal, hot dogs, buns, and sodas in the cart, you can observe that it should be a great weekend for a cookout. If you see the person in front of you staring at the tabloids, you can make a comment about the "Martians who landed the back yard", or the latest movie star scandal.

The weather, an attractive accessory (tie, belt, shirt, pin, earrings, haircut, smart watch, smart phone, cool shoes) a current news item, the book someone is reading, a headline in the newspaper rack; can all stimulate a conversation. Most of the time, you'll get a good response. While the conversation may end when the line moves, it still will be good practice, and an interesting experience. And who knows? You could make a new friend.

Stay in Your Own Head; Not Theirs
Wherever you have a conversation with a potential friend or date, remember to stay focused on what you think. It is very easy to worry about what the other person is thinking about you and forget what you are observing about them. You are pretending you can get into the other person's head: you're projecting your insecurities onto the other person and pretending to look at yourself through the other person's eyes. There are two things wrong with this. First, there is no way you can accurately guess what the other person thinks. Second, you're wasting time, when what you should be doing is paying attention to your own opinion of the other person. Stay behind your own eyes, in your own head, and using your powers of observation and evaluation to gather information about this person. Your job is to know what you think of them; not to worry what they think of you.

Invite Interest/ Show Interest
Susan, 35, and I were discussing her dating experiences. "It's like the school lunchroom," she said, "if you have a baloney sandwich, and your friend has a great-looking PBJ, and you want some of his, you have to offer to share half of your sandwich first." It's a great image for the way you let someone know you're interested, and to return her interest. A big smile and eye contact held for a couple of beats toward someone who is nearby will signal "come on over, I want to know who you are." Keeping the tennis match of the conversation going, and not dropping the ball, asking questions or making observations that invite an answer (you can say almost anything and add "what do you think?" to the end of it) and including the new person in the conversation if an old friend shows up, signals that you're interested.

Compliments on what someone is wearing let him know you're paying attention. But, compliment people only on clothing, intelligence, good ideas, clever comments. If you comment on personal attributes such as beauty, weight, facial features or being in shape, you'll sound shallow. Such comments, though meant as compliments, can easily sound too nosy or insulting. Questions about what she thinks, how he feels, what she likes to do, what kind of friends he has, are very flattering, and invite people to stick around and get to know you. When your new friend states an opinion, it's more inviting to ask some follow-up questions that say "tell me more" than to immediately counter with your own opinion. Everyone wants to be understood, and nothing is more fascinating than being the object of someone else's interest.

Body Signals
You can either invite or exclude with your body posture, too.

- Turning away excludes, turning toward invites.

- Crossing arms on your chest, or putting an arm on the table between you as a barrier excludes, relaxed, open posture invites.

- Looking beyond someone to watch others is rejecting. If you're interested in the person you're talking to, you won't scope out the other people in the room: this is another great reason to look around for a while before you begin talking to anyone, you can get this search out of your system.

- Leaning toward the person shows interest, but could get too invasive and intense. If the other person leans back, you're leaning too close.

- Leave enough space between yourself and the other person. Don't touch total strangers — once you know each other a bit, then being close and touching are inviting — before you know each other, they're threatening. If the other person moves away, you're overdoing it.

- Nod your head occasionally as the other person talks, to let them know you're agreeing, understanding, paying attention. Smile a little to reassure them that you're enjoying the time. Be aware of your facial expression. Don't frown in concentration or anxiety; it will look as if you don't like what you're doing.

Drop the Right Hints

Your conversation, mannerisms and reactions are like cue cards that tell the other person how to respond to you, and what to talk about. If you don't like talking sports or business, then be very careful not to bring them up, and change the subject when they do come up. The brand-new acquaintance you're talking to is looking to you to supply the clues about what you want to discuss. If you are interested in politics, drop a hint: say "I've been following the news, and I'm very interested in the latest campaign." If you're a movie buff, mention the latest picture you've seen, or a classic you just rented or streamed. The other person will usually pick up on it, if he or she knows anything about it. If she or he lets it drop, that is also a communication.

In addition to letting other people know what you want to discuss, you can also let them know what you're interested in knowing about them. The more you can draw a new person out, the more you learn about her character and lifestyle, which is also how you'll tell if he's a suitable partner.

Interviewing

What most people don't know is that, to be successful, you can, and should, interview everyone you talk to. People give tremendous amounts of information about who they are, how emotionally and mentally healthy they are, their likes and dislikes and their relationship histories.

In workshops on How to Meet New People, I explain to the whole group how to interview, and then I set a scene: You're sitting in a Laundromat, waiting for your clothes to dry, and someone is sitting next to you. Find out as much as you can about that person, *without being obvious about it,* for five minutes. When the time is up, I ask people to stand up and introduce each other, telling what they learned. It is always astounding to the entire group, including both introducers and introduced, how much people can learn about each other, without interrogating, in just five minutes.

Here's how to interview:

- Have a mental list of topics you want to cover (for example, friends, family, past relationships, favorite activities, current events, movies).
- Conduct a tennis match conversation, tossing the conversational ball back each time you get it by inviting the other person to respond.
- Pay close attention to everything the other person says. Do not let your mind wander.
- Look for clues in the conversation. For example, if the person makes several references to drinking: "we went out for a couple of drinks... we were having a drink... I had a couple of glasses of wine." It could be a danger signal. If he or she describes past relationships and puts all the blame on partners, it could be a warning sign. "...history is important. If Madge was a real bitch who took him for all he was worth, and Heather was a total basket case who just used him and abused him, and Fiona, well, she was one crazy lady - he wouldn't be surprised if she were a drug addict or worse", writes columnist Cynthia Heimel, "then I'll hide under the house until this guy leaves." On the other hand, if he or she talks fondly of good friends and fun times, that's a positive signal.
- Focus on your companion. Be very interested and intrigued by what he or she is saying. Your friend will feel understood and cared about, relaxed, and positive about your talk, and about you. Don't avoid talking about yourself, but try to say just one small thing, and then toss the conversation back to your partner, by asking a question such as "Have you ever (done, felt, seen, thought) that?"

- Try not to repeat meaningless stock phrases, such as "know what I mean?" It sounds as if you're not really thinking and not entirely present.
- When the conversation is over, carefully review everything you learned. If it's a person you won't see again do this just for practice. If it's someone you're interested in, make some notes, so you won't forget.

It will take some practice before you feel completely comfortable interviewing. Try it on some willing friends first (someone in a support group would be ideal. You can learn together). Then, try it on new people you meet just for practice (don't worry about whether you want to date them, just practice interviewing them). Once you have done it a few times, you will be amazed at what you can learn, positive and negative, about the person your interview. That person would be equally astonished to know what they revealed.

Attentive Speaking

To conduct your subtle interview successfully, use *attentive speaking,* a simple and highly effective technique that will help you communicate better with everyone you know. It means paying attention, not only to what you are saying, but also to how the other person is receiving it. If you watch carefully as you are talking, your listener's facial expression, body movements, and posture all will provide clues (looking interested, fidgeting, looking bored, eyes wandering, attempting to interrupt, facial expressions of anger or confusion, or a blank, empty stare) will tell you a lot.

The following guidelines will teach you how to observe your listener, and gather information. This is especially effective if the other person is not very talkative, is reluctant to disagree or object, is a strong, silent type, is easily overwhelmed in a discussion, or is passive.

- avoid monopolizing the discussion or boring the other person (if he or she looks overwhelmed, bored or distracted, you're talking too long)
- keep your listener's interest in what you have to say, (ask a question if you're losing his or her attention)
- understand when you are misunderstood, (facial expression is not what you expect)
- gauge your listener's reaction (notice facial expressions, body language and attentiveness)
- Know (by facial expressions, body language and attentiveness) when your listener is distracted, stressed or preoccupied.

Guidelines for Attentive Speaking

1. *Watch Your Listener.* Be careful not to get so engrossed in what you are saying that you forget to watch your listener. Keeping your eyes on your listener's face will indicate you care if he or she hears you, and increase your listener's tendency to make eye contact and listen more carefully.
2. *Look for Clues in facial expressions.* (a smile, a frown, a glassy-eyed stare) body position (upright and alert, slumped and sullen, turned away from you and inattentive) and movements (leaning toward you, pulling away from you, fidgeting, restlessness). Rejecting body language may mean you have talked too long.
3. *Ask, Don't Guess.* If you get an unusual or inappropriate response, (you're giving a compliment and he looks confused, hurt or angry; or you're stating objective facts and she appears upset) ask a gentle question. For example, "I thought I was giving you a compliment, but you look annoyed. Did I say something wrong?" or just "Do you agree?"
4. *Give Your Listener a Choice.* If your listener looks distracted or bored, invite opinion: "What do you think?" or "Do you see it the same way?"

5. *Be Aware of confusion.* A blank or glassy-eyed look, or confusion, means overwhelm or confusion. Again, ask a question: "Does this make sense?" or, "Do you have a question?" Sometimes, just pausing gives your friend enough room to ask a question or make a comment.

Paying close attention to how your words are landing can give you lots of information about the person you are getting to know.

Openers

Starting a conversation is often anxiety-producing, but you need to learn how: you can't always wait for the other person to approach you.

This is where your first half hour of observing comes in handy. You can make a comment about what people have been doing, the food, the music, or just "It's a lovely (party, evening, house, picture, view) isn't it? Or compliment something about the person: "What a great (tie, pin, dress, shoes, T-shirt, color, design) I like it because..." He or she will probably say "thank you", but also respond with some information. If the answer is, "Thank you, I got it in Paris", you've hit pay dirt. With a few questions, you can keep him or her talking all night about Paris....

Your opening comment shouldn't be a line like "what's a nice _____ like you doing in a place like this?" Or "what's your sign?"... That's not how to make a good impression. Keep your statement simple, and as relevant to the time, the place, and the person you're talking to as possible. Ask a question about where something is, or who someone nearby is, or what's been going on.

- If your companion gives you any information at all, respond to it. Let him or her know you're listening by making an interested comment.
- If the person doesn't respond to your first or second try at conversation, move on to someone else.

- If you're at a party or gathering where groups of people are having conversations, it is OK to go up to them, listen a bit, and if you know something about the topic, join in.
- If you know someone else at a party, you can ask for information about someone you don't know, or even ask for an introduction.

Try on a Persona: Practice Being the Femme Fatale, the Hero
If you have trouble being comfortable in a group of people, try on a persona. Pick a character you saw in a movie, or a stereotype like the femme fatale, the Superspy, the diplomat or corporate raider and get into that character before you go in. Acting as if you're someone else won't work for long, but it may be just enough to get you past your initial anxiety and into the mood for a party or social event, and it can be fun.

Picture Your Successful Relationship
Nothing will motivate you better before going to a new event than spending some time before you leave home visualizing the relationship you want to have. Picture yourself surrounded by good friends, happily with someone, falling in love, spending your evenings and weekends with someone you enjoy being with. Take the time to remind yourself why you're doing this, and you will feel a lot better about trying new things.

Your Ideal Lover

If you want to find the right person, it definitely helps to have an accurate picture in your mind. If physical appearance is important to you, make that part of your picture, but don't forget that the most important qualities you are looking for are internal. Take the time to do this effectively with the following guidelines:

Ideal Lover Exercise
1. Set aside some time when you can be undisturbed for about half an hour. Sit in a comfortable place, with soft

background music if you wish, and have a pad of paper and a pen nearby.

2. Close your eyes, and picture an ideal partner. He or she may be a composite of the best of your former relationships, favorite story characters, movie heroes, TV stars, members of your family (your Dad's sense of humor, your Aunt Sara's kindness) or other people you have known in real life. Take your time picturing exactly what this partner would be like, and change the picture as many times as you want, until it feels right

3. Use all your senses: sight, smell, touch, hearing, and taste in the picture. What scent does this person wear? Does he or she simply smell clean, like soap? What does he or she look like? How is this person dressed? What does this partner's voice sound like? How do the kisses taste?

4. Picture you and this ideal mate doing things together. What are you doing? Where are you?

5. Do this a few times, until the image of the kind of person you consider ideal becomes clear.

6. Once the image is clear, open your eyes and write down the most important characteristics of this ideal mate. Fix the image in your mind, so you can remember it even when you are not doing the exercise.

Once you take the time to create a clear image, you can bring it up in your memory to remind you of the reward you are aiming for when you're meeting new people. If you have found yourself in difficult relationships, this is one way to re-program your radar.

Make a Relationship Map

Visualizing the relationship you want with this ideal partner is the next step. Making your map will help you focus clearly on your goals for partnership, and also encourage and motivate you. Don't worry about your map; it is strictly for your own benefit, and it is only necessary that you understand what represents. You can change it as much as you want, until you get your picture exactly the way you want it.

Your Relationship Map

- *Preparation:* You'll need art materials or a drawing app or program, and a good source of pictures and advertisements that you can cut and paste, as well as several photos of you and others in your life. If you enjoy drawing, you may want to dispense with the pictures, and draw your own. If you're a computer whiz, then computer art may be the way you do this; if not, old-fashioned paper and paste works very well. You can also add solid objects, pieces of cloth or jewelry, tokens and keepsakes that are meaningful to you. Colorful, graphic pictures are powerful subconscious stimulants, and the point of this exercise is to help to focus your subconscious on your ideal relationship.

Look through magazines, emojis or computer graphics, and find pictures that represent your ideal relationship. If you'd like to do outdoor activities, choose pictures of couples biking, hiking, swimming, etc. Find a picture that represents a comfortable home life, such as a roaring fireplace, or a lovely table setting. Find symbols of love, laughter, good communication, teamwork, sexuality, and happiness. Find as many pictures as you like, to represent what you want to create in your relationship.

- *Creating Your Picture:* Arrange or draw these pictures on your paper, or drag-and-drop them, in a way that suits you. Place a picture of yourself front and center of the page. You can even put your own face on a picture you found. Arrange and rearrange and adjust your collection of pictures until the final result pleases you. When you are finished, the picture should be a clear enough visual representation of your relationship that you are reminded at a glance of what it means. Don't hesitate to redesign your picture, if you get better ideas of how it should look. When you have it complete, stand back and take a look to see if it you like it. If not, play with it some more, if it is, paste things down, and find a place to put it where you can look at it when you want to.

Birds of a Feather: Meet Friends of Friends

Nothing can help your life be more fun than making friends. Doing things with friends makes everything more fun. And, as the statistics show, more people meet their mates through friends. There's good reason for this. Once you make friends with the kind of people you want to bring into your life, you will gain entry into their social circle, also. People tend to socialize mostly with people who are of a similar type; educated people socialize with other bright people, sporty people have sporty friends, friends tend to be within the same socio-economic level, and friends often have work and activities in common. You can take advantage of this, if you keep in mind that every new friend you meet is not only valuable as a friend, but also brings a whole network of possibilities.

Never Miss a Party

In order to take maximum advantage of the network, take advantage of every party invitation you get. Anything from a pool party to a movie night to a formal dinner at a friend's house is a great opportunity to meet even more friends. Somewhere in this haystack of connections is the needle you are searching for: your perfect relationship

Let Your Friends Know

Everyone you know, especially those who are coupled, will be eager to help you find a great partner, if you let them know you're willing to accept their help. Put out the word about what kind of a date you're looking for. If a relative or friend of someone you know appeals to you, let your friend know. He or she will either save you time by letting you know the appealing person is off limits or has problems, or they will arrange for you to meet. What better way to meet someone than if you're both invited to a party at a good friend's house?

If a co-worker you like goes out to lunch with someone interesting, ask a few questions. You may find out that person is available. However, if you do meet and date the friend or relative of someone you know, be a bit careful. Make certain you treat this particular date with even more courtesy and care than usual, even if you decide you're not interested. If you anger your date, you'll upset your friend. For example, don't say you'll call and then forget.

Make New Friends, Keep the Old

The point here is to *add* to your circle of friends, not to *change* friends. The adage "Make new friends and keep the old; One is silver, the other is gold" applies here. No one can replace your long-time friends; and there is no need to. They can still occupy the same place in your life they always have. Hopefully, some of these new friends will stay around and become old friends, but some will not. Visualize the people you know circling around you as planets revolve around the sun. Some are very close by, some are more distant, yet all of them can be in the same system. In the same way, you can be closer to some friends than to others, but all of you are connected. It can take a long time; sometimes many years to create a deep and lasting friendship. They are called "gold" because they are a valuable and precious resource. Newer, less well known friends can be valuable also, even though they may come and go. You can still have good times with them and meet others through them. They can add lots of fun to your life. They are "silver:" not quite as precious, but still to be valued.

Network like Crazy!

Anytime you are around one other person, you have access to a potential network. Don't hesitate to connect with that network, if you have any opportunity. Invite your friends to invite *their* friends when you're going to coffee, a movie, out to brunch or over to your house. Ask everyone you know for their favorite places to go for fun, and for recommendations to classes, organizations, church groups and sporting activities. See if you can join in when you hear a group of people are going camping, on a picnic, or to a dance.

One way to get to know someone slowly or to indicate you're interested in a person strictly as a friend is to do things in groups. That, too is a great chance to network. All your friends are part of your social network, and they connect you to many more networks. It is said there are only six degrees of separation between you and anyone else on the planet. That means that someone you know, knows someone else, who knows someone else, etc. until that chain connects you with the person (for example, a movie star or the President). So, perhaps to find your ideal mate somewhere on the planet you have to form a chain or a network of at least six connected people. The bigger your network is, the easier it will be. If you network, you'll find your true love, and have fun doing it.

You'll Have More Fun than You Think

We discussed all the reasons to dread dating, and to feel insecure when you think of it. When you actually get out there, if you follow the instructions and guidelines here, you'll find that it is not difficult or unpleasant at all. Because you are following a successful process, you'll meet a lot of new friends, and date some very nice people. The guidelines will keep you far away from disasters, and will maximize your odds of being successful.

Not Just Looking for a Date, but Enjoying Life

You can make this process simple and pleasurable or difficult and painful, simply with your attitude and outlook. If you strain to meet your goal, focusing on one narrow definition of success, and are impatient and disappointed when you do not meet it immediately, you will have a struggle. If you resolve to enjoy the process, have a sense of humor about your mistakes and about the things that don't turn out as you wanted them to, you will have fun, and you will find what you're seeking more easily.

In short, approach this as an exercise in enjoying life and getting out of your own way. Spend some time every day being grateful for what you have, and balance that with some time focusing on the most efficient and enjoyable way to get what you want, and you will succeed and have fun in the process.

Exotic Places to Look

Another way to maximize your fun is to find innovative and unusual places to meet new people. Get your local news app, listen to reviews, and when you hear of something that interests you, don't be afraid to check it out. For example, here in Long Beach, we have the Aquarium of the Pacific, and it invites volunteers. For people who are interested in the ocean and ocean life, volunteering is a great way to meet other people with similar interests, have fun doing it, and have a great subject for conversations!

Travel can be a good way to meet people, also, if you don't mind running the risk that your new friend may live far away. Joining a ski club which has ski trips, or a kayaking group which does whitewater trips, help out an archeological dig for a summer vacation, or even a gourmet cooking group which travels to exotic locales to focus on the food, can be both a great travel experience and a wonderful way to meet and get to know someone. Are you a train buff? Would you love to pet a koala, or ride an elephant? Fulfilling these wishes can also be an exotic way to meet new, potential partners. The internet can be a way to travel without leaving home or spending a lot of money, and also a way to meet people. Internet dating services may charge a fee, but there is no charge for most Bulletin Boards, Chat Rooms or online discussion sites.

Becoming the Person You Want to Meet
To get the most possible benefit from finding love today, use it as an opportunity for personal growth. If your intention is to become the kind of person you'd like to date, or better yet, the kind of

person you'd like to fall in love with, you'll use your mistakes and disappointments as sources for growth.

While this may not be the sort of fun you have in mind, it can be extremely rewarding and satisfying. Psychiatrist Abraham Maslow, the founder of Rational Emotive therapy, studied man's happiest and most memorable moments, which he called *peak experiences*. He said that they occurred most often in people who were *self-actualized:* meaning they had worked on and learned how to be the best people they could be.

A more modern researcher, the University of Chicago professor Mihaly Csikszentmihalyi, calls his study of "the psychology of optimal experience" *flow*. He says achieving flow, "...means paying attention to what is happening around you so that you notice things, care about what happens, and forget yourself in the process. Whatever you are doing becomes very absorbing and interesting." This kind of absorbed interest is the same state of mind you use when you're learning. So, having a beginner's mind, focusing on learning whatever you can, and paying attention, as this book recommends, also increases your chances of enjoying and feeling good about your experiences.

To change your focus from negative to positive, whenever something goes wrong or you make a mistake, take the time to learn from it by analyzing it. Write down what happened, and come up with three things you could have done to avoid or correct the problem.

This Is Your Life: Now, Single, Fun; You'll Miss it when You're Mated
Above all, remember to appreciate your life today. Don't fall in to the trap of thinking you'll be happy later, when you find the person you're looking for. Every moment of your search is not wonderful, but a lot of it is fun. You are single; you have the freedom to do whatever you want, without having to take a partner's feelings or wants into consideration. It's that freedom that long-time married couples miss. This is your chance to meet everyone you want to

meet, to do whatever you want to do, to try out your fantasies, to make sure that when you do finally settle down, you won't regret it or miss your freedom any more. Meet and date enough people to be sure you know, when you choose one, that it's the right choice. Learn everything you can about yourself as a single person, so when you have a relationship, you'll know what you like and don't like as an individual, without your partner's influence.

Make the most of every day and every opportunity while you're dating today. The following chapters will present more step-by-step information to help you be successful, to keep yourself safe, and to get the most fun out of the experience.

CHAPTER FOUR

A Confident Start

What Is Dating About?

OK, you've explored your anxieties, you've prepared yourself, you're ready to go.... do what? The best dating is about accomplishing something in addition to simply meeting friends, having fun and meeting a partner. It's about something very specific and special to you. What you need to know is, what do you want to create in your life by meeting new people?

What Are You Looking for?

Hopefully, you're not doing this simply because you think you should, or looking for just anyone to date. Like any other activity, to be successful, meeting new people needs to have a purpose: to suit who you are, and to accomplish one or more specific goals.

Fun?

Of course, you want your time spent meeting new people to be fun, rather than a drag, but what is fun to you? How will you know how to have fun with someone else, and how will you know if they're having fun with you? In this chapter, we'll explore what makes things fun for you, and how to find or create an atmosphere that helps you to have fun.

Serious Relationship?
Are you looking for a committed, serious relationship? What does one of those look like? Do you know if that's what you want? Does it sound like an impossible dream, or too scary to think about? The kind of relationship that works well for you now might be different from the ones you've had before. You've changed and grown, and hopefully, you've learned from your experience. I don't recommend that you commit to any relationship that will not make you happy. If you discover what kind of relationship you require, and how to recognize another person who wants the same thing, you don't have to be afraid of being trapped or disappointed. This chapter shows you how.

Sex?
It's entirely possible that you're happy with your solitary life, and you want to date strictly to find one or several sex partners. You think: "I just want to date: I'm not ready for a relationship." It's a legitimate thing for you to want, if you're clear about it. The danger is that you won't really be certain this is what you want once you are dealing with actual people. On the other hand, most people who date are hoping for some sort of sexual connection, with varying degrees of commitment implied. It's essential to know how much sex and commitment are involved in what you are looking for, and whether sex implies commitment to you, and at what point you consider sexual contact OK. Thinking it's OK to have sex after a date or two, and thinking that you should wait until you have a monogamous commitment or are married, are vastly different conditions, and need to be clearly understood by both you and your partner.

Companionship?
Perhaps what you really want is a companion, someone to do things with and spend time with, and commitment and/ or romance are decisions you'll make later. "Having friends has been of major importance to me since high school, when I had virtually none."

writes Suzanne in an Internet chat, "my community of friends is even more important to me than a lover...." Friendship is not only an essential support system for you as an individual, friends also enhance and support your relationships. As Anais Nin wrote: "Each friend represents a world in us, a world possibly not born until they arrive, and it is only by this meeting that a new world is born." Knowing what kinds and degree of companionship is most satisfying to you will also help you know what you're looking for.

You're Just Bored?
Whatever the reason you are single and searching, you have probably spent some time alone, recovering from a loss. At first, the only thing you want to do is hide out at home, but, after a while you'll get restless. Feeling bored is a sign that the bandages are coming off, you're healing, feeling stronger, and getting ready to try some new things. Heed your boredom and get out there... you'll feel better doing new things, even the ones that don't turn out, then you will by sitting around doing nothing.

How Important Is It?
Meeting new people is far more important than just the search for a relationship. Through your search, you'll accomplish several things:

- learn how others see you
- make new friends
- practice communication with a variety of people
- sharpen your ability to evaluate people you meet
- have fun
- cultivate some new interests
- practice your relationship skills

A Major Part of Life?
The importance you assign to finding a new relationship will dictate how much time and energy you want to put into it. If being in a relationship is very important to you then it makes sense to put a lot of effort into dating successfully, if it's less important to you,

having a good time and making friends may be of greater importance. The significance with which you view relationships, friends and fun will shape your attitude and approach. It's part of determining your style.

If friends and fun are more important, you will focus on meeting lots of people, getting to know them whether they're eligible or not, and enjoying group activities and more theme-focused events, such as sports, classes and hobbies. Once you get your network of friends in place, you'll be content with it. If you are clear that your goal is a committed relationship, you'll still do those things, because they're a great way to meet people, but you'll be more focused on gathering in-depth information about individuals, and making one-on-one connections.

Secondary to Work, Kids, Family, Hobbies?
The phase of life you are in will also affect how important dating is for you. If you are at a crucial point in your career, if you have younger children, if there are elders or others in your family who need your care, or if you are deeply involved in some avocation or art that requires a lot of time and energy, you will have less time for meeting new people than if you're less involved. To make a realistic plan, you must know what is most important in your life. If your life is busy, it will probably be necessary to schedule some time for dating, and stick to the schedule, or you will find that it never happens. Also, if you are feeling too stressed or guilty because you're neglecting other important things, you won't enjoy your time off.

Try this: List your major responsibilities and activities. Then, rank them in order of importance. Add dating to the list, wherever you think it belongs in the ranking. Making the list will show you how much time and effort you can spare for finding love. When you evaluate where dating ranks in your priorities, you can avoid stress and guilt by devoting appropriate time, not too much or too little. With a little thought, you can also combine some of your priorities with dating-related activities. For example, if you have children, you can join some child-parent activities that give you time with your kids, and also the chance to meet some new people who are also parents. Or, if you like to be active, you can experiment with new sports, different leagues or events where a number of teams get together, and meet some new people.

Celebration +Appreciation = Motivation

The energy you bring to dating will make a big difference in your results. You can maximize the energy you have in two simple ways. (1) Celebrate each of your accomplishments, and (2) appreciate yourself for who you are, your style of doing what you do, and what you're learning as you meet new people.

What Will Make this Fun for You?

The first section of this chapter, exploring what dating is all about for you, can help you appreciate your style. If you look at your motives, your circumstances and your desires honestly, without criticizing them, you will get a sense of what your search style will be, and why. There's no need to give yourself a hard time if dating is low on your priorities, just accept that your life is busy right now, and adjust your expectations accordingly. You can still have a good time and be successful meeting new people, even if you only have limited time to do it. In fact, understanding that you have a tight schedule will hopefully cause you to choose your activities wisely, and may even make you more successful. On the other hand, if you haven't much going on in your life at the moment, and it feels a bit empty, use that as a chance to combine meeting people with exploring activities and opportunities you want to add to your life. Either way, begin looking for the positive aspects of who you are and your style, and capitalize on them.

Celebrate the Small Steps

Celebration always creates motivation and energy. Every time you acknowledge an accomplishment, you are encouraged to try for more. If you have to wait for the grand prize, you'll lose energy before you get there. Celebrating your small accomplishments can make the difference between feeling like a failure because you didn't meet Mr/Ms Wonderful tonight, or like a success because you went out, met some nice people and had fun.

As you develop your personal style, break each step down into its smallest components, and celebrate them. For example, if you've decided to take a class, you can break down the process of choosing the class and signing up in to very small steps: calling for a catalog, reading the class descriptions, making a choice, finding out how to register, registering, attending the first class. Each of those tiny steps can be celebrated, if only by crossing it off your to do list, calling a friend to discuss what you did, or breaking open a can of soda and toasting yourself.

Celebrating this way may sound strange, but you'll find if you do it, you'll be a lot more energized and you'll procrastinate less. We all thrive on recognition and rewards, even from ourselves. Of course, the bigger the step you've achieved, the bigger the celebration will be.

If you enjoy games, celebrate your small accomplishments before your big success happens, with score points. Develop a point system, based on how difficult things seem: 2 points for making an info call, 1 point for talking to a friend, 5 points for speaking to someone you don't know. Keep a mental record of your points for the evening, and have chart at home for tallying your score. You'll find a point system helps you stay focused on your real goals. For example, if you go to a party, and you know you'll only get a point each for speaking to the people you know, you might be more motivated to try speaking to strangers.

Keep your overall goal intact while you do whatever you can do right now and you'll stay on track better, and be more efficient at seeking your goal. The point system is one way to reward yourself for doing the most effective things, focusing on the points will automatically keep you on your program. There are other ways, too. For example, reminding yourself what you are looking for before choosing an activity or saying "yes" to an invitation, or reviewing your goals just before attending an event can prevent you from self-defeating behavior. If you know your goals are to meet new people, you won't spend the whole evening huddled in a corner with people you already know, or accept invitations that waste your time.

Acquire an Arsenal

To really get out there and have a good time, you need ammunition: your own personal arsenal of tricks you can use to help you through whatever comes up.

Clothes and Make over

Your appearance is the first impression you'll make when you're meeting new people, and while your character and personality are much more important, a proper look will smooth the way. If you're great with clothes, and love to put outfits together, you're all set. But, if like most of us, you feel unsure about what to wear and when to wear it, you'll benefit from some advice. If you have a friend or a relative who looks well-put-together, ask for some help. If your friend is willing, you can go through your wardrobe, and get help with mixing and matching, which clothes look good on you and which don't and what to wear to which event. Just a few outfits, put together from clothes you already have, are all you need to get you where you want to go. The clothes you wear should reflect your personality as well as suit the atmosphere you are in. Dressing too casually for a formal occasion, or overdressing when everyone is casual, is not a crime, but it can make you uncomfortable, and take away from your fun.

Hair and (if you wear it) makeup should be neat, tidy and appropriate to the activity, also. Looking more or less like the kinds of people you want to meet is the best bet. If you stand out in the wrong way, you may get attention for it, but it may be the wrong kind of attention. When you know you look your best, and your appearance is appropriate to what you're doing, you'll feel more secure and more relaxed.

Support System
Your support system is a very important part of your arsenal. Good friends and helpers can help you with appearance, what to say and do, how to answer questions, and give you honest feedback about your appearance and approach. Enlist friends and family members, as well as any professionals you might need, to help you be prepared. Podcasts and webinars can also be very helpful.

Communication Techniques
The more you know about communication and conversation, the better your chances of really getting to know someone. If you use communication skills at work, don't forget you can use those skills in your social life, too. If you feel inadequate in communicating, try practicing with your friends; ask a friend role play with you. You can imagine you're at an event, party or class you're going to, and practice how to approach your friend and begin a conversation, or practice having the friend approach you. If you run through several scenes, you will feel a lot more confident when you are in the real situation. If role playing with friends doesn't answer your questions, try taking a class, webinar or learning communication techniques online. You will not only learn how to communicate; you'll also be creating an opportunity to meet some new people.

Equipment
If you're going to meet people in clubs, it's a good idea to have a post office box and voice mail which do not give your home address. You may want to be able to be reached without giving out your home phone or address. You can print up personal cards, including your name, your post office box, voice mail, and/or e-mail address on your computer or you can have them printed cheaply and quickly online. These cards come in quite handy when you're meeting people for the first time. They have the advantage of giving

the correct spelling of your name (you can omit your last name, if you really want to feel secure) and giving you the security that the other person has the correct number, so if you don't get a call, you'll know it's a choice, and not a mistake. There's more about equipment in Chapter Eight.

Dating Can Be Fun

If you think of what you're doing as making friends instead of dating, it will sound a lot less intimidating, and make it easier to change your old habit patterns. When you focus on attending an event to have a good time, you'll feel less anxious.

Making it Fun

Whenever you are in a new place relax, talk to some people who seem easy to meet (whether you'd like to date them isn't important; they can be older, younger, any gender or orientation. You're just meeting people.) Focus on enjoying whatever is there to enjoy.

- If you're attending a class, concentrate on the lesson or the activity, and don't worry about who's there for the moment.
- At a party, talk to anyone who seems easy to approach.
- If you're playing or watching sports, concentrate on the game.
- At a committee meeting, the PTA or a volunteer group, get the work done.
- On a hike or camping trip, watch for plant and wildlife, and enjoy nature.

Once you are at a function or event, you'll have a lot more fun if you forget about dating, and participate fully. You'll enjoy what you're doing, and because of that, you'll be far more attractive. That's why it's important to do things you can enjoy in the first place.

What Are You Interested in Learning?

"A non-drinking shy person is going to wither very quickly in the garden of singles' clubs and a classical music lover is unlikely to meet a kindred spirit in a jazz club," writes sex columnist *Ask Isadora* Alman, "forcing yourself to go where you feel like a fish out of water will give you just cause for not going out again. While learning new things and exploring new places is the very essence of growth; you might as well be realistic." The area of your interests is the place you'll find people you want to meet.

Aside from finding a partner, what interests you? Are you an Astrology or Tarot buff? Do you like to play or watch golf, tennis, basketball or other sports? What about the theater, the arts, politics, photography, science, bridge, books, computers, crossword puzzles, computer programming or computer art, model (or full-scale) airplanes or boating? The possibilities are endless. If you follow your own interests, you'll automatically meet people you can have fun with, and who have something in common.

How you follow those interests makes the difference: If you just buy a ticket and go to a baseball game, you are not too likely to meet anyone. (The love of your life could just happen to have the next seat to yours, or be standing in the hot dog line when you go, but the odds aren't good.) However, if you get involved in a booster club, or find a group of people who enjoy playing or going to games, or even meet with a group to watch games on TV, as long as there are enough of the right kind of people for you, you'll have a great chance meeting some friends and eventually making a serious connection. A sports bar that's playing the game can be a great place to meet people, but be aware of the alcohol consumption. If you just take photos, you'll have nice photos. If you go to a photography class or group, you'll have the photos, plus a chance to meet others you can click with.

To turn your interest into a dating opportunity, just find a way to meet other people who love the same things. Find a group or a class on the subject, and you'll automatically find others who love it. In this computer age, you can search for others who like similar things. Through them, you can also network, and learn about new resources and more people who share your interest.

What's Fun about You?

What do your friends like to do with you? What do they seek you out for? Do they like to come to your place for dinner? To go to the beach? To talk? To go walking or bike riding? To work on projects together? Would your friends say you have a good sense of humor? The people who know you best want to do what they have the most fun doing with you. They think of you first when they want to do that activity, because you help make it enjoyable. Pay attention when your friends seek you out, or compliment you, and remember what they consider important about you. Also, consider the personality qualities you like about yourself: Knowing what people enjoy about you is valuable for two reasons: First, it's good to remind yourself of those positive attributes when you're feeling anxious or unattractive. Second, you will know what qualities to display when you're meeting someone new.

How to Be Irresistibly Attractive

The most attractive people are friendly and interested, but not too interested. Being relaxed and enjoying what you are doing, chatting in a friendly manner, cooperating with the people around you are all appealing. When you're interested in someone, smile in that person's direction, perhaps chat a bit, but after a short time, turn your attention somewhere else; give your quarry time to think about how pleasant it was talking to you. If that person is interested, he or she will find a way to get next to you again.

In the ideal situation, you'll be near this person repeatedly, in some kind of scheduled fashion, as in a class or a group which meets regularly. Each time you meet, give the other person a big smile, and mention something from the last time you met. For example, "Wow, you changed your seat today, last week you weren't so close to the front of the class." Or, "You always look so nice; I thought that (tie, scarf, vest, sweater, shirt) you wore last week was neat, but this one is even better." Or, "I noticed you were taking notes, and there was something I missed from the last class. Can you look it up for me?" The person will feel flattered, noticed, and remembered. After the greeting, go on about your work. Let your quarry make the next move, as in the tennis match approach from Chapter Three.

This kind of gentle, flattering interest, with no pressure, is the most attractive. It is irresistibly attractive in that it produces a positive, elusive image in the other person's mind. Behavioral psychology research shows that intermittent reinforcement is the most effective type. That means, giving a reward (your big smile and greeting) and then leaving a space with no reward causes the subject to become fixated on when the next reward will come. It is undeniably attractive and intriguing.

Putting all these clues together, using the information you've gathered about what you like to learn, what you have to offer, and how to hook someone's interest will help you decide where when and how your personal hunting process will work. Of these criteria, the most essential is finding the right places to go. Finding places where you can learn something of interest means finding people who share your interest.

Different Ages, Stages and Attitudes
At different stages of life, we have different approaches to dating, and different reasons for it

- *Twenties:* In their 20s most middle-class people used to be focused on finding a marriage partner and having children. Today, the younger generation of middle-class daters tend to be more focused on career and postponing marriage and childbirth. If you are in this group, you are most likely looking for a partner to enjoy time with, but not yet feeling ready for a serious commitment or a family.
- *Single Parents:* If you are a young single parent, you may have decided you just want an occasional companion, with

no intention of co-parenting or living together, or you could be considering whether the person you're dating will be a good step-parent.

- *Thirties and Forties:* After 30, if you're educated and well-employed, you probably are more career-focused, establishing yourself financially, investing in property and retirement accounts. At this stage, you're more interested in commitment and partnership; most likely you want a partner with whom to build a future. If you want children, this is when the urgency to start a family is acute.
- *Middle Years:* Dating in your 50s and 60s may mean you have lost a long-term relationship, have children in college or older, and be looking for someone with whom you can enjoy traveling and spend your weekends with. You'll probably feel more like settling down and pursuing a healthy lifestyle.
- *Retirement*: In these later years, your dating focus may be able to be less focused on creating your security, and more on enjoying it. Leisure pursuits, community activism, and enjoying your grandchildren may be on the top of your list.

Whatever your stage in life, and whether your personal life journey exactly matches these, your age and circumstances will certainly influence what you're looking for in a date.

The Importance of Slowing Down

If you find someone you want to date, give the dating a chance, and don't get too serious. By going slowly, and taking time before settling down to one person, you have a chance to learn more about yourself and the other person. When you do decide to focus on one person, if you go slowly, you'll give your relationship a chance to grow and go through stages, and reach its full development. In my counseling practice, the biggest single mistake I see people make in relationships, the one that results in disaster, is being too much in a rush to choose one person and settle down. Or, to just stay with the first person who seems to get along with you. To give yourself a choice, you need to date for long enough to meet and get to know several people. The experience of interacting with several people will teach you about how you react to different situations, and which problems you bring to every relationship.

Observing yourself in relationship with several other people will give you new insight into your personal relationship dynamics. Once you have observed the differences in relating to several people, you will be able to make a more solid choice of special person.

Focus on Fun and Friendship
To keep things going slower, and give yourself a choice, keeping your focus on fun and friendship is ideal. You can get to know many people at once by attending group activities and going out with groups of friends. Seeing how the people who interest you interact in a group can tell you a lot about their character and relationship skills. A focus on fun keeps the interaction light and allows you to learn more before the relationships get too serious.

Whether you're male or female, to keep your relationships in balance, especially when they're brand new, make sure you don't do all the calling, all the planning, all the talking, all the giving, and all the chasing. Make a move to show the other person you're interested in being friends, then sit and wait for your new friend to make a move in return. For example, make a phone call to invite him or her for coffee, or to join a group going to the movies, and then, let him or her make the next invitation.

This is often difficult to do, because the natural tendency, if you're interested, is to be aggressive. But being too active in the relationship may push the other person away, or may disguise a lack of enough interest on the other person's part. To use our tennis metaphor, don't keep hitting balls over the net if they're not returned; and if you never hit the ball, but always wait for the other person to do it, you aren't playing a very good tennis game, either. It's essential that you do your part, because passivity is easily interpreted as a lack of interest. The tennis metaphor is helpful, because if you compare what has gone on in the relationship so far to a tennis game, you will quickly see if you've been either too passive or too aggressive.

Keep It Slow and Casual

When you meet someone who excites you and even returns your interest, you may be very tempted to focus solely on that relationship, and stop looking. This is neither wise nor safe. When you meet someone who returns your interest, the most effective thing you can do is continue making friends and trying new things, while getting to know this new person. Include the new person in on some of your plans, but not all, and make sure, until you have a chance to really get to know more about him or her, to be around other people when you're together.

This may sound too cautious, especially if you're sexually turned-on, or eager to develop a relationship. But, please keep in mind that you've just met this stranger, no matter how good it feels. Seeing this new person interact with others, getting feedback from your other friends about your new date, and taking your time to get to know each other is much safer, more sensible, and more effective. When you find the kind of quality person you're looking for, you can laugh about your caution later. But, if you find out that this person has a problem history, you will be very grateful you waited.

As I write this, I have an acquaintance who has a very impressive job, is attractive and seemingly successful, but also has a history of many broken marriages, children with several partners, and a problematic legal history. Yet this person is about to be married another time. I often wonder why the new partner hasn't found out about the history, or even worse, has discounted it. Appearances are deceiving. If a person is unknown to you, and your friends don't know him or her either, be very careful. It's extremely easy, in today's mobile world, to hide a frightening background. Also, whatever you do, don't ignore a person's problem history, or make excuses for it. Check things out carefully before you leave yourself vulnerable.

The Un-date

To keep things going slowly and smoothly, learn to have *un-dates*, get-togethers which will give you a chance to get to know new people, without the commitment and interest implied by an actual date.

Un-dates Are:
- going out for lunch
- going out for coffee
- a walk in a public park
- meeting at almost any place like a museum
- taking a class together
- sharing the cost of a concert or movie

When you share expenses, it signals that you are going out as friends, without the extra pressure of dating: it's an *un-date*. To set this up, you can say, "Can we meet for coffee?" or "I'm going to the movies Friday, would you like to join me? Tickets cost about..." After going out in this casual fashion for a while, you can always change the intent by asking your new friend on a real date, and paying for the meal or outing. One appropriate phrase to use is: "Please come to the movies Friday, *as my guest*" or "I'll treat." A date is a more formal occasion than a friendly get-together.

Group Un-Dates
Another way to keep expectations from getting too high and things from going too fast is to invite your new friend to join you and other friends for a meal, a movie or an outing. If you meet somewhere, and there are other people involved, the outing will give you a chance to get to know each other; and it will give you a chance to observe your new friend interacting with others. When others are around, especially if you don't pick up your new friend, it will automatically feel like an un-date.

Working with this new acquaintance on a class project, a volunteer committee or a political or church event will also surround you with others, and provide a similar opportunity to learn about each other and to watch the interaction.

Un-Date Times and Places:
- Certain venues almost automatically feel like un-dates; because of the time of day, or the setting. If the setting is very informal, and not very romantic, your companion will not be as likely to think you're on a date.
- Lunch, because it's in broad daylight, especially if it's in a less-expensive restaurant, feels like an un-date. Be warned, however, a picnic lunch, lunch at your apartment or in a very dimly lit place will feel more date-like.
- Coffee, because it's inexpensive, fairly brief, and around people also feels less romantic. It does not involve the time, money or energy commitment that goes into taking someone out to dinner.
- Talking via phone or video, because it's not face-to-face, and thus creates some distance in the conversation, is a kind of contact that is not seen as a date.
- The library, because it's functional, and you probably need a reason like, "I'll help you find another book on that subject if you'll meet me at the library after work."
- A walk, because it's very informal, and out of doors, feels more like a friendly act than a romantic one.
- Any activity that does not appear to invite romantic contact or involves limited opportunity for being alone or intimacy is a good non-date.

Providing opportunities to get together with someone you want to know better in the above ways will reduce the tension, limit the possibility of sexual involvement and keep you safe until you're sure you have found someone you want to become more intimate with.

Create Flow: Ease in Communication

To create a relaxed flow of communication between yourself and another person, demonstrate *disinterested interest*. That is, be interested in what her or she has to say, and fascinated by details of his or her life, but do not display any concern about whether those things will mix well with your needs and/or wants. This is too soon to insert yourself into the other person's picture. You can chime in with things that are similar in your own experience: for example, if he or she says "I go walking every morning, I find it's great exercise" You can say, "I love walking; I like to walk on the beach in the evening." Avoid "That's too early for me" which makes you sound as though you're competing or comparing, or inviting yourself along.

In your own mind, you can make those judgements and comparisons you need to make to discover whether this is the kind of person you want to be close to, but aloud, just be politely enthusiastic for some part of your new friend's conversation. The conversation will flow better if you leave plenty of space for the other person to give you information, without halting the flow by objecting, interrupting or challenging anything that's said. Your questions should be designed to elicit more information, as in "You went to Finland? I've always been curious about that part of the world. What is it like?" which encourages the flow, rather than "You went to Finland? That's too cold for me" which stops it.

Don't Be a Drag: Following, Not Leading

Here's the place to begin following the relationship, and not leading it, as we discussed in the last chapter. Allow things to develop any way they want to, as long as you're taking care of your basic safety, and not doing anything that feels like a bad idea. Do give yourself a chance to find out what your partner likes, wants to do, wants to talk about, wants to spend time with. Don't insist on doing it the way you want to do it. For the time being, go a long a little bit. Make your own suggestions, but also go along with your partner's suggestions, (as long as they fit your criteria for going slow). By doing things your friend likes, and seeing how your friend responds to your suggestions, you will learn a lot about how a relationship would be with that new person.

Above all, take you time and observe carefully who it is you're dealing with. Be aware of making assumptions (he's well dressed, he must be a good guy; or she's lovely, she must be emotionally healthy) because you'd really like them to be true. The more you relax, go slow, and allow your partner to relax and reveal as much as possible. This is the best way to be safe and not sorry.

Know Yourself: Who Are You?

What do you want in a partner? Most people don't know. They want someone nice. The same person wouldn't buy a car, a new outfit, or a head of lettuce with such vagueness. I see so many men and women choosing people to date with less thought than they'd put into choosing a turkey for Thanksgiving dinner. At least for the dinner, you *know* you're getting a turkey!! A person you're initially attracted to can turn out to be ineligible because he or she is not verbal enough, too verbal, too assertive, too passive, uncooperative, addicted to some substance or habit, dishonest, unreliable, uncaring, demanding, not intelligent enough or any number of personal quirks or traits you cannot manage to live with. Many of these traits can fall within normal ranges, yet be unacceptable to you. Couples fight over smoking, eating habits, money, sleeping habits, religious differences, pets, children, friends, holiday and family traditions, house cleaning, and time schedules.

Finding the proper match in a person to date begins with knowing clearly who you are. As a unique individual, you need more than a cookie-cutter idea of who you want to date. Are you gregarious or shy? Physically active or more sedate? How much sex do you want? How much closeness, how much space? Are you a loner, or a people person? These traits point the way both to where you meet people and which of them to focus on. "One of the pleasures of being a grown-up is that you can now pick your own friends on the basis of your own choosing," writes Isadora Alman, "wanting an outgoing gregarious friend while you are shy and withdrawn is not an impossibility. Such a balance might well be to the liking of both of you. The point of any good relationship is that both people in it enjoy and benefit from it."

If it seems premature to examine your life in such detail when you haven't even met a suitable person to date, remember that being clear about your goal will affect each decision you make throughout your dating experience. The following information and exercises will help you define who you are, and then who you would like to be with, more clearly.

Selective Attention: How it Works

As human beings, we are equipped with a miraculous bit of brain acuity known as *selective attention*. This mental marvel allows us to unconsciously focus on whatever we deem important to us. For example, if you have a crush on someone who drives a blue Toyota Prius, you will probably notice similar cars driving by, whether you want to see them or not. It can be quite distracting. This same ability shows up when you scan a page and your own name, or a foul word, jumps out at you.

What you may not know is that selective attention governs which people you notice, also. If a parent was an alcoholic, you may find yourself able to pick out the one alcoholic in a room full of people. You naturally seem to gravitate to that. If a parent was angry, or passive, that's who you'll notice today. This can strongly affect the kind of people you are drawn to. Selective attention can cause you to notice people who feel familiar, who remind you of family members, and who have similar patterns of behavior; even if your parents, siblings, or other relatives were not particularly good to you or for you.

The good news is; you can change this selective attention to focus on the kind of person you actually would like to meet. To do so, it is necessary to let go of the familiar as a criterion and to develop a new awareness of what really works for you. If you have had a series of relationships that have all resulted in similar problems, or that have just not made you happy, then you're probably operating on old programming. You've never taken stock of what a healthy person is; you've just been blindly looking for someone who would love you. The way you re-focus selective attention is to get a very clear picture of your new objective, your quarry, which begins with knowing yourself accurately. The following exercise will help you know who you are in a relationship.

Know-yourself Exercise
Mentally step back and look at yourself as objectively as you can. Keep in mind that this is a fact-finding, not a fault-finding mission. Imagine a typical day in your life, and think about what you do: morning/evening routines, meals, work, play and general lifestyle. Answer these questions as though you are responding to an interviewer who is hanging on every word!

Waking up
- What are you like when you wake up in the morning? Are you slow and groggy, cheerful or quiet? Are you organized or haphazard? Do you have a regular routine that never varies, or do you get yourself ready differently each day?
- Are your clothes laid out the night before, or do you have a sleepy interlude at the closet deciding what to wear?
- While you're getting ready, are you relaxed or tense? Are your movements slow or fast?
- Do you follow a routine in the AM, such as exercising or meditating?
- Do you like to sit and read the paper, or do you pare your morning time to the bare minimum, and sleep in?
- Do you eat breakfast at home, on the run, at work, or not at all?

Mornings can be crucial in a relationship. Most of us are more natural and less rational first thing in the morning. You express your personality in your morning routine, and it is vital information for you and your potential partner to have. Couples who begin their mornings in harmony have a better chance of continuing to enjoy each other throughout the day.

Work
- Is your work creative, challenging, stressful, artistic, boring, detail-oriented or technical?
- Do you work with the public, co-workers, or alone? Is teamwork required? Do you supervise others?
- What is the mix of people you work with? Is it comfortable for you?
- Do you like your job or profession? What do you like best about it? If you don't like it, what would you rather do?

Your work, and how much you like it, says a lot about your preferences, your strengths and weaknesses. For example, if you enjoy a people-oriented job, you may be very outgoing and want to have many people in your private life. Or, if contact with the public is stressful, you may prefer lots of time alone when you're not working. Your stress level, travel schedule, work brought home, and other factors will also impinge directly on your relationship. You have also learned a lot of skills at work that you might want to bring into your relationships, such as how to communicate as equals and how to work together to solve problems.

How important is your work? If it's more important to you than your relationship, or periodically takes precedence, you need to acknowledge this. It's possible that your career occupies a primary place in your life. If personal time is something you only get when your career permits, you'll need a different partner than if you make your home life a priority. Knowing this beforehand can save a lot of struggle and disappointment.

After Work

- What do you usually do after work? Do you come right home and relax? Do you take a nap so you'll have energy for the evening? For dinner, do you cook a special meal or microwave a frozen dinner? Are you active: that is do you run off to classes, meetings, rehearsals or workshops? Or are you quiet, preferring to spend your evenings watching television or reading, then relaxing in the hot tub?
- Do you usually pursue creative hobbies, like writing, painting, building things in your workshop, rehearsing with a little theater group or playing an instrument?
- Do you work out at the gym, play a pickup game of basketball, jog, go to softball practice, rollerblade or do some other type of exercise after work?
- Do you get together or go out with friends on weeknights? Do you spend time with your children, your family, your pets?

Weekends (or days off)

- When do you wake up on weekends? What is your weekend morning routine like?
- Do you eat differently on weekends? For example, do you barbecue with the neighbors, eat out more? cook at home more? Take the kids out for burgers? Go on picnics?
- Are you involved in organized weekend activities, like sports or group events, or is your activity more individual and spontaneous?
- Do you attend church, synagogue, temple, meditation sessions?
- Do you volunteer time at political, social or charitable events?
- Do you putter around the house or yard a lot?

Like evenings, weekends are usually considered couple time. Look at your current weekend and evening lifestyle to see what activities you want to share with a partner.

General Lifestyle Quiz
The following questions can help you to develop an overall picture of who you are and what your wants and needs are in a relationship.

- Are you more organized or more spontaneous?
- Are you a very neat housekeeper, who cleans regularly and thoroughly, or are you sloppy and haphazard about it? Do you pay someone else to do it for you?
- Do you like a busy environment, with lots of stuff on the walls and knickknacks and mementos on the tables and shelves? Or do you prefer a spare, clean uncluttered environment? Do you like decorative frills or straight clean lines. Mid-Century Modern or early Victorian?
- Are you around people a lot by choice?
- Do you spend more time with your own gender, the other gender, or with mixed groups? With one person at a time, or several? With old friends, family, new acquaintances, your children, former lovers?
- Do you spend much time alone? Do you like solitude?
- Do you have pets? How much of your time do you spend with them? Will a partner have to like pets, too?
- Do you have children? Do they live with you, either full or part time? Are they grown? How often are they around? How close are you to them?
- Are you artistic? Do you often have a creative project going? Do you spend a lot of time at it?
- Do you have a sport or hobby that consumes lots of time, energy, space and/or money?
- How are you with money? Are you responsible? Are you very detailed, or more casual? For example, do you

balance your checkbook every month, to the penny, or do you get a vague idea of how much you have left from the instant teller balance? Do you ever bounce checks? Are you meticulous about paying bills, or do you sometimes get late charges? Do you like doing the accounting chores (paying bills, balancing checkbook) or do you wish someone else would do it?

- Is food important to you? Do you like to cook? To entertain? To dine out? Do you follow a special or vegetarian diet? Do you have food allergies?
- Do you like intense conversation? What about?
- Are you careful or casual about your appearance?
- Are you spiritual or religious? Do you attend a church, synagogue, temple, retreats or meditation sessions?

You in Relationship

- What do you want to do in your relationship? It should be somewhat similar to what makes you happy now. Examine your fantasies of being in relationship to see that they actually suit your lifestyle.
- If you spend lots of time home alone, a fantasy of being coupled with someone who is the center of a social circle could be very unrealistic.
- To get an accurate picture of what really would work for you in a relationship, examining your history, and comparing it with your wishes for the future, is a good place to begin.

Where You've Been: Analysis of History

Make a list of your major past relationships. Go back through the know yourself exercise, and make notes about what you did in these relationships about each of the categories: How you spent weekdays, weekends, mornings, etc. Divide these notes up into what felt good and worked well, and what didn't. If there's something you did, such as read the paper together in the morning, that you really loved, make a note of it. If there's something you did, such as have to wait for your partner every night to eat dinner, or always get stuck doing the dishes, or have to be quiet on the weekends while your partner slept late, or be wakened earlier than you wanted to by a noisy partner, make notes of that, too.

Where You're Going: What Will Be Different
Using the know yourself exercise information, plus the analysis of your history; condense the details into a list of the kind of activities you want to do in your new relationship. This list should include the most important things you want to do, for each time of the day and week.

What Really Counts in a Partner?
Now that you have clarified your idea of who you are and what you like to do, it's time to focus on who you want to be with. Doing this will set your selective attention. Using the following information will help you figure out if the attractive individual you're considering is a good match. This research is precisely the reason I suggest you focus on friendship and take your time. It takes a while to know the deeper attitudes and values of someone new.

Beauty Is Only Skin Deep
When thinking of the kind of partner you wish for, it's easy to let your focus be on what the person will look like. There is a great emphasis on looks in our society, especially in the media. Keep in mind that you're looking for a person with whom you'll spend a large portion of your time. What he or she looks like will fade very quickly; you won't even notice it very often. Your partner's deeper characteristics such as: personality, intelligence, values, integrity, warmth, sense of humor, little quirks, and ability to cooperate and solve problems will soon come into sharp focus and be much more important than mere surface looks. It is these characteristics, rather than hair or eye color, stature or appearance, that you need to focus on to be successful. Let's look at some of the basics:

Temperament, Sense of Humor, Intensity
Your partner's attitudes will be central to the question of whether you and this person are compatible. You have examined your own attitudes and temperament: what kind of person will be compatible with who you are?

Are you a relaxed person? If so, would you do best with someone as relaxed as you are, or do you need someone with a bit more energy, to offset your calmness? Opposites often attract: that is, if you're very verbal, a quiet person might be appealing at first. But, after a while, opposites can be grating: when you've been together a while, the other person's quietness may be irritating to you.

One way to see what kinds of attitudes are most compatible is to look at your past relationships, your friendships, and your family relationships: Which kinds of people do you tolerate better for long periods of time? Which do you enjoy being around for a short time, but soon want to get away from?

Take a look at these relationships and evaluate the temperament and attitudes of the people you most enjoy being close to. What do they have in common? Do you tend to enjoy warm, talkative people? People who are quiet and allow you plenty of space and privacy? Fun people who are always ready to go out? Solid people you can trust and count on? Think about what personality types you have around you, who you spend most of your time with, and who may just be fun on occasion. Taking the time to examine these relationships can open your eyes in terms of who you could really manage a long-term relationship with, and who would be initially attractive, but soon become irritating or boring.

Intelligence, Verbal/tactile/visual/auditory
The match between you and your partner in terms of intelligence and communication styles will have a large effect on the ease of your problem-solving and teamwork. You can certainly learn to communicate with someone who has a different style than yours, but ease of understanding comes with similar styles. Again, look

around at friends and relatives and evaluate who feels easiest for you to understand and who seems to understand you best. Familiarize yourself with these traits so that you'll recognize them when you see them in a stranger.

People use their senses differently, which affects perception and communication. Just as you have your style of living, and your preferred way of dress, you also have certain ways of absorbing information. There are three ways we acquire information: auditory (hearing), visual (seeing) and tactile (touching). Once we absorb these impressions, we then use our imagination to compile an impression. Most of us learn by using a combination of these avenues, and your particular combination becomes your perception style. People receive information in different ways; we are auditory, visual, tactile and imaginative in different proportions. That is, words (sounds), pictures (sight), touching and imagination are more or less important to you depending upon your perception style. Sensory preference refers to the senses you primarily use to receive information with the deepest understanding. For example:

Sensory Preference
- *Auditory/verbal:* If you absorb information mostly through listening to words, and you think in words rather than pictures, your style is more verbal and auditory, and not very visual. You will be more likely to think in words than in pictures, and you know you have understood a new idea when you can explain it clearly. If you're auditory, you enjoy talking, lectures and audiotapes, you listen for the words of popular songs, and you may enjoy listening to the radio. You'll probably use a phrase like "I hear what you're saying" or "It sounds like..." to mean you understand someone. Sexually, an auditory/verbal person is turned on by talking and be talked to.
- *Imaginative:* Are you a daydreamer? Do you often practice scenes in your imagination, such as running over a job interview or a discussion in your head several times before

actually doing it; or replaying past scenes with people? If so, you are used to understanding via your imagination. For you "I wonder", "Let me think about it" and "I can see it in my mind's eye" would be common statements. Sexually, fantasies are big with the imaginative person, and lots of play-acting.

- *Visual:* If you understand better when you see things, and you tend to picture ideas rather than think them in words, you probably know you've understood something only when you can picture it. If someone tells you about their vacation, and you've been to the same place, you'll get a visual picture of the whole discussion. Such visualization videos, watching someone else or seeing diagrams and pictures are probably the most effective way for you to understand. You may say visual things like "I see" meaning I understand, or "see that?" meaning, do you understand? Your turn-ons probably include clothing, mirrors, videos, etc.
- *Tactile:* If you lean toward the physical, and you are a tactile (touching) person, you understand best by doing, tinkering with things, and you know you've understood when you feel it more than see or hear it. Walking through a new idea, acting it out physically, using things you can touch, work well for you. For you, "I feel it," or "I've got it" are ways to say you understand. As lovers, tactile people are usually sensual, like to touch and be touched, and not as verbal or visual.

Knowing your own sensory preference, and observing the styles of others, will help you communicate more effectively. For example, if you're asking someone to feed your cat, and you are verbal, but they're visual or tactile, take them through your kitchen, open the cupboard where the cat food is, and let them do it themselves while you watch. If their style is auditory, you can write instructions, or just explain, and they'll get it. Try it a few times; you'll see the difference it makes.

Spiritual Issues/ Ethics/ Standards

While similar religious backgrounds or belief systems aren't' required to make a relationship work, they are also basic things that can aid your understanding of each other. You should at the very least be able and willing to talk to each other about the deeper meaning of things. If a spiritual or religious point of view is very important to one of you, a partner must be able to respect and listen to that point of view, without dismissing or ridiculing it.

Spiritual differences are one of the things that are easy to ignore and gloss over when the relationship is new, but become more and more difficult over time. If one of you has a spiritual point of view, it will affect many things you do, and decisions you make. You must be able to come to an understanding about these matters.

For example, Sue is not willing to watch violent or very negative movies; she believes they are unhealthy for her emotional/ spiritual well-being. Her husband loves action/adventure films, although he doesn't like gory movies. He goes to see the violent ones with other people, because he respects that it's not something she wants to do. They have different, but compatible religious beliefs; they can discuss how they feel about a matter, and come to a mutual understanding. He meditates while she prays, but they both understand the value of devotion.

Similarly, Tom is Jewish, and Jane is Protestant, and they were married in a mixed ceremony with both a Rabbi and a minister. They have mixed the two religions, Tom has learned to cook some of the ceremonially significant foods he loves, and Jane helps. They light Sabbath candles, but Tom goes to temple on Friday nights and Jane to church on Sunday mornings. They often attend each other's' services and special functions, and they enjoy teaching each other and comparing notes. They plan to teach their children the basics of both faiths, and allow them to choose when they get older.

In these ways, a couple with different beliefs can blend, but it takes thought and effort. Similar spiritual beliefs can give you a mutual understanding and also provide structure to your relationship that requires less effort.

Financial Condition; Wants and Needs
Most of us don't consider it very nice   to care about the financial status of a person we're seeing, and, indeed, it's inappropriate at the beginning. But, if the relationship is going to become serious, your different money situations and attitudes will rapidly become a big issue.

You have looked at how you are with money in the know yourself exercise. Now, look at your imaginary partner. Do you want someone who is very careful, invests wisely, plans for the future, and doesn't want to spend much today? Would you do better with someone who is less concerned, and more willing to be spontaneous with money? Are you looking for someone who does money the way you do, or someone to balance you? That is, if you're thrifty, do you want someone as thrifty, or do you want someone who, while responsible, will help you loosen up and enjoy spending a bit from time to time?

I don't recommend looking for a partner to rescue you from money woes, because often the price you pay is very high, but, if that's really what you want, at least you can be honest with yourself about it. Money is one of the top three things couples fight about, along with sex and power. Money, in fact, can often be used to control a partner in a relationship. Couples who fight about big money issues are not happy. Take the time to sort out your money issues before you get too serious.

Similarities and Differences
Neither similarities nor differences in themselves will make or break your relationship. The challenge and stimulation in a relationship arise from the places where you're different, and the

trust, comfort and security between you grows from your similarities. Neither differences nor similarities are bad in themselves. But, if you get too much difference your relationship will feel like lots of work, and if you get too much sameness, it will feel smothering and boring. Understanding how different you are and which similarities and differences you want will help you achieve the proper balance.

- *Tidy or Messy:* Many a relationship has foundered on shoals of clothing tossed on the floor, or cluttered table tops and funky bathrooms. A tidy person with a messy partner is not a good match, unless you both have a great sense of humor about it, and can negotiate well. For example, a messy person may love gardening, working on the car, and tinkering around, while the tidy partner does the housecleaning and the dishes. The untidy one may even love to cook, if you will clean up. Often, sloppy partners are great with children, pets, and in bed. So, there can be many compensations. But, if you get together with one of these, don't expect any transformation. The housework will be yours, or you'll pay to have it done. "Love seems blind to personal habits, writes Miss Manners, "and people who can't tell the difference between a house and a hamper inexplicably manage to attract people who alphabetize everything short of their children."
- *Expression Styles:* People tend toward physical expression or mental expression. While many people achieve a balance of both, you'll want to have an idea whether you and your partner are physically and mentally well matched. A computer nerd or a bookworm, who likes being inside and values mental stimulation, may have difficulty being matched with a physical person who has to have vigorous exercise on a daily basis, and can't sit still for long. Think about how much and what kind of physical and/or intellectual activity you'd like to share, and discuss your

preferences with potential partners. Like most differences, these can be worked out, if you're both flexible enough about what you want. But, if your preferences are too different, you might be disappointed later on. A person who has been longing for someone to hike with and camp out may not be able to reconcile with an intellectual who prefers reading and quiet discussions with a partner. Or, someone who loves classical music and opera may not bond well with a die-hard sports fan.

- *Social/quiet:* One reason the opposites attract dictum arose is that social butterflies and quiet corner sitters are often mutually attractive. The social life of a gregarious person can be very seductive to a shy one, and the quiet, composed space of a reserved person can be very refreshing to the party person. Again, the differences can be worked out, but you must be aware that you are different, and that your differences, charming now, may become less acceptable later on. A gregarious person can feel stifled and trapped by a quiet one, and the shy person can feel overwhelmed and highly irritated by the more social one.

- *Activity Levels and Overload:* Although you've examined your personality differences, you may not have thought about how much activity is enough, and how much is too much. If you're both busy, involved people, combining all your activities may be overwhelming, and deciding which ones to share, which to do separately and which to eliminate altogether may be necessary. Some activities may be essential to you, such as physical exercise, political action or hours of meditation or practice of a skill or talent like throwing pottery, studying music, Karate or Tai Chi. Others may be more easily let go. If you find that there is too much going on for the two of you, remember to sort through what feels vital to you and what is easily let go. Even if you disagree about how important some particular activity or involvement is, if it's important to you, stick to your guns. If you let go of something you love to keep this partner, you'll resent it later, and that will create tension in your relationship.

Your Past Partners

You have considered the people you are closest to in order to discover the personality traits you are looking for in a partner. Now we will focus on your past relationships, to discover both what worked and what the problems were. Doing this should help you become more clearly aware of how your selective attention caused you to choose, and what aspects of that automatic attraction you need to challenge.

Past Partners Exercise

This exercise is much like the process a therapist would do with you if you asked for help in transforming your relationship patterns.

- *Positives:* What Was Good about Him or Her: No matter how difficult you may have thought a relationship was, in the beginning you were hopeful, attracted and excited. Write down each major relationship in your past, (or use the list you made in the Analysis of Relationship History). Under each person's name, list the most positive and attractive qualities you saw in that person. Be honest with yourself here. If the attraction was an affluent lifestyle or a hot body, list that, too: even if you'd feel differently today.

- *Negatives:* What Was Not Good about Her/Him: Now, on the same list, write down the negative qualities. What eventually led to the end of the relationship? If it ended due to your partner dying or leaving, perhaps ill health or inability to commit would be one of the negatives. Take your time and remember what about each person drove you crazy, or made problem-solving, having a good time, or just being together difficult. These negative traits can be anything from a serious character flaw such as addiction or dishonesty, to a small habit, such as not putting the cap on the toothpaste, or not being affectionate enough.

- *Problems:* What Relationship Difficulties Did You Have: What were the problems in each past relationship? If you had only one relationship, and few problems, then look back at other relationships with siblings, parents, friends or co-workers where you had difficulties. Analyze what went wrong, and what part was played by you and by the other person. These problems can be anything from money arguments to workaholism, to violence to too much interference from in-laws or family.

- *Solutions:* Were You Able to Solve Them? If you solved some problems in the course of your relationship, pay particular attention to how you both did that, and what each person did to contribute. This may be a bit difficult to remember, because once a couple truly solves a problem, the whole issue tends to fade into memory and be lost. But it's an extremely important indicator of negotiation and behavioral skills you already possess, and you can build on the things you remember.

- *How?* For example, did you learn how to talk things through without getting angry? To sleep on the problem for a day or two, until you both calmed down, and then solve it? To keep current with each other, so resentment didn't build? The skills you learned in past relationships, even though the partnership didn't last, are still useable in relationships you have now.

- *Why Not?* If you were unable to solve some problems, or if you never understood what the problems were, write that down, too, and analyze it as thoroughly as you can. Here are the clues about what you need to learn or change, or what skills you need to look for in a new partner.

- *How Does the Next Partner Need to Be Same/Different?* Look at your written examples carefully. They represent your relationship patterns until now. When you take the time to analyze and compare them, you can see the patterns emerge. Once you see both the good and bad patterns, make a list of the qualities and characteristics you want in your next partner. Take the best of what you had before, add the missing qualities from your know yourself exercise, and condense it into a description of the person you're looking for.

Take enough time with this, and use your sensory preference.

- If you're a visual or imaginative person, visualize this partner, and picture the two of you going through a typical week, seeing the details of your time together.
- If you're verbal/auditory, read aloud what you've written, or describe your ideal partner and relationship to a trusted friend.
- If you're tactile, walk through your home, picturing your new partner there, and acting out what you'll do together.

You and your partner may not be the only people you have to consider when thinking about a relationship. If you're a single parent, the next chapter will help you manage dating.

CHAPTER FIVE

But I'm a Single Parent

If you're a single parent, you probably have so little free time that meeting someone new seems an impossible task. Single parents are dating in unprecedented numbers, so if you're looking for a counterpoint, another single parent to date, you'll find one.

Single parents are forced to be efficient, however, just because they don't have endless time to waste hanging around waiting. As a responsible single parent, you'll also want to be very cautious about whom you date and eventually bring home; for the safety and well-being of your child(ren).

Dr. Romance's Guide will help you be efficient, and answer some of the most-asked questions single parents have about dating.

You Are the Parent

If you are the person who has children, you may feel guilty or unsure about whether romance is OK. Of course it is, as long as you do it responsibly. Your children, however, should not be disrupted by your adventures. The age of your children will influence your opportunities and choices, as will shared custody.

If you share custody with the other parent of your child, and the children are gone some or most of the time, especially on weekends, which is of course the most obvious time for you to date. Since your free time with your children is somewhat limited, you'll want to be with them when you can.

If the other parent only takes the children occasionally, or not at all, then you need to arrange for the children's care when you're out meeting new people. There are some ways to meet new people with your children along, and we'll cover those, also. Until you know the new person well, it's advisable not to share your experiences with your children.

Your Date Is the Parent

If you are dating a single parent, circumstances are different. Depending on the children's ages and on how much of the time your date has them at home; their presence can change your experience a lot. A single parent is not as free to do whatever he or she wants, and must consider the children first. If you do not have children of your own, you may not understand some of your date's concerns and issues. This chapter will help you learn what is appropriate when dating a single parent.

You Both Are Single Parents

If you are a single parent, there are several advantages to dating someone who also has children:

- You understand each other's issues, needs and pressures.

- Once you have established a good connection, both of you and your children can do things together (see cautions about bonding below).

- You can share parenting information and issues.

- Sudden problems, like a sick child, will be taken in stride.

- Your partner probably likes and understands children.

- Budget constraints are probably mutual, and will be understood.

The Basics of the Dating Parent
Dating as a parent requires not only finding someone you like, who

likes you, but also someone who is comfortable with your children. The children add extra dynamics to the situation, which can be frustrating, but should not be ignored or overlooked.

If your children do not like someone, or your date is uncomfortable with them, you can continue to date, but it is advisable to keep your new romance separate from your children, which will severely limit your involvement if the children are young. Your children should not know you are romantically involved until the relationship is serious, and by that time, they should be comfortable enough with your new friend that it won't be a problem.

If you pressure your children to like your date, or go too fast for them to get comfortable with the situation, you are asking for a lot of trouble. By following the rules here, you will make sure your children are comfortable with your new date, and that things go smoothly.

Safety and Sensibility Issues
Your first priority, for yourself and your children, needs to be your safety and theirs. Today's society is very mobile, and it's easy for people who are not savory to hide their backgrounds. That is a major reason I suggest getting to know people as friends before dating them. Group activities, daytime activities with the children along, being in public places, and establishing someone's character before being alone (and especially before leaving your child alone) with them is the safest way to go.

Keeping yourself safe, as in the guidelines in Chapter Two, becomes even more critical when you're a parent. Of course, your child's safety is just as important. Don't be too quick to get into a car with a person you don't know, or to be in a stranger's home, or have a new acquaintance in your home, especially when your children are present. Keep in mind; if you put yourself in danger, it affects your children's lives, too.

Meeting other single parents at PTA, church, and school or sports events is a great, non-threatening way to begin. The public setting provides safety, and a chance to get to know the other person, to find out what others think of him or her, and to meet his or her children, which will tell you some things about the kind of parenting they have gotten. Your children meet the person as the parent of other children, not as your date, so it's much less threatening and ominous to them. There is less pressure on everyone.

Who Keeps the Kids?

So, when you do get to know someone well enough that you'd like to move to the next step and begin individual dates, rather than group activities, what do you do with the kids?

This depends largely on how old the children are, what arrangements you've made for their care while you work, and your custody and child care arrangements.

It's easiest, as I said above, to date on nights when your kids are with their other parent, but if that's not possible, and if your children are very young, infants to early school age, you'll need a baby sitter, unless grandparents, relatives or their other parent will take them. It is not a good idea to try to entertain a date at home with the children there, even if they're supposed to be asleep. You'll be distracted, and the kids shouldn't know too much about your dating life. To minimize childcare expense, create a village: a network of other single parents, and parents of your child's schoolmates, who will trade off letting your child stay overnight, if you invite theirs to stay with you at another time. This way, you can share child care for free.

Being Clear about Priorities

As a parent, you have priorities, and so do your children and the person you're dating. Respecting everyone requires having boundaries, making sure everyone understands them, and sticking to them.

- *With the Kids:* If your children are small, they have a right to be primary in your life. They should not have to feel that appropriate attention is taken from them, and given to your new relationship. They should not have to compete for your time, attention and affection. This will not be easy, because as a single parent, your time is probably already at a premium. The older your children are, the less time they need from you, and the more freedom you should have to date as you want to. As soon as they're old enough to understand, explain to your children that there is a certain amount of time you need to call your own. You do not need to explain about being lonely, or needing a new partner. This should not be their problem. Once you have arranged for appropriate care for them, you can do what you want with your own time, including date someone. However, your romantic arrangement should not bleed over into your other time. Keep your family and your dating separate until you are sure you are ready to blend them responsibly.

- *With Your Date:* Your date needs to understand the importance of your family, and to make the choice to explore what can develop with you, but not to disrupt your family life. From the first moment you realize that you're interested in a person, that person should understand that you must be a parent first, and a companion second. The person you are dating should also understand your rules about parenting, and how much say he or she has over your children's behavior. As a friend, your date has no authority; but you have authority to make sure your children treat your friends politely. If the relationship goes well, and your date's friendship with your children grows, these priorities may change a bit, and they will also change as your children become adults, but that should happen slowly. When you begin to form a new family, then your new partner can gradually begin to have some say over your children's behavior, but that requires a lot of discussion and problem-solving among all of you.

126

Who Meets Who, and When

When you introduce your date to your children, (unless you meet as parents of children of similar ages, as discussed above) let it happen naturally, and don't make a big deal out of it. There's a fine line to tread here, because if your relationship gets serious, it's vital that your date and your children get along, but you don't want your children to get bonded to someone who's not going to be around. They've already lost one intact family, so more people coming and going in their lives is not a plus. It's alright for casual friends to disappear, but not for people who are closely bonded. Because you're a parent, you and your date each have responsibility not to put the children through difficulties they have not asked for. Be sure you are both adult enough to maintain at least a friendship if you decide to allow your date to get close to your children

Your children, especially when they're small, shouldn't be subjected to a revolving door of people coming and going in their lives. It's fine to have them meet acquaintances and say "hello", but not to get close to person after person who soon leaves. There is enough loss in life that we can't control; it isn't necessary to add unnecessary losses to the mix.

Kids Shouldn't Have to Compete

As a single parent, you have your hands full, but your children should never feel they have to compete with your adult relationships for your time and attention. It is fine to ask a child to play for a while so you can talk to other adults, but not to neglect the child in the process.

Too many single parents drag young children around to adult functions where they don't belong, feel out of place, and have nothing to do, because the adult feels guilty about leaving them with a sitter. The child doesn't get time with the parent, and is really being disrespected and disregarded. While it's appropriate to teach children of school age how to behave in adult settings, it is not appropriate to drag them everywhere you go. If you cannot keep an appropriate balance between the attention you give your children and that you give your friends or dates, you may need to consult a family therapist to learn some skills.

Decisions as a Family

Your child deserves to have his or her opinions respected. You don't have to agree or go along with what your child wants, but you should at least know what those wants are, and your child should know why you're overriding his or her preferences. Regular family meetings, where everyone including the children expresses feelings, negative and positive, and all of you work together to solve problems, can help a lot.

Begin family meetings as soon as possible, before any of these dating issues even come up. Choose a time when everyone can get together weekly, and suggest to your children that you order pizza, or provide something they like. At the meeting, everyone (including you) begins by stating three good things about others in the family, Then, each person gets to mention one thing they want to improve, and what they want to do to make it better. Small children will need help until they understand, but they will catch on quickly. Even you and one child can do this. If your date begins to be a long-term relationship, the family may decide to invite him or her to some family meetings. It's a great way for everyone to begin to work out blending someone new into the family.

Boundaries and Guidelines for Everyone

In relationships, when boundaries are clear, everyone knows what is expected of them, and what the consequences are of crossing the line. If you set boundaries early, and are consistent, everyone will feel respected and secure.

Children aren't the only ones who need rules to follow. If the adults involved (you, your date, your ex, grandparents, friends) do the right thing automatically, they are following their own internal boundaries, but if their habits don't work for you and your children, you'll have to inform them of yours.

Ages and Stages

Appropriate boundaries vary a lot according to the ages of your children. Infants are too young to understand, but as they grow, more and more rules are needed, until they are mature enough to make good decisions on their own. Understanding and living according to rules of behavior early in life gives a child the foundation he or she needs to self- regulate behavior as a teenager and young adult.

- *Toddlers:* Toddlers begin to understand simple rules as soon as they understand language. They are learning from you, so keep in mind that your behavior is teaching them. In terms of your romantic life, your toddlers only need to know they're going to be taken care of while you are gone, and perhaps, after you are certain your date is of good enough character, to learn how to say "hello" to your adult friend, and the very beginning rules of politeness, when you all spend time together. As the relationship grows, your toddler and your date will have to form their own connection, and you should give them enough space to do that, once you're sure your relationship is reliable enough to be worth it, and your new friend is safe to be around your children.

- *Elementary School Age:* Should they happen to meet your date (which is not at all necessary at first) all your school age children need to know is that you are going out with a friend. They should be required to be polite and sociable when they meet your friend, (after you feel sure it's a worthwhile enough person). As the relationship grows, if you begin to think it will last, you will want to go on outings with the children and your date. A ball game, a trip to the zoo or the movies, a picnic in the park, will give everyone a chance to get acquainted. These are all chances for your children to learn the socially acceptable forms of politeness and good behavior. You are responsible for discipline and organization, and your date should not be involved in these issues yet. Don't inform your young children that you're dating.

- *Teens:* Dating and romance issues get more complicated when your children are pre-teens or teenagers. They will understand the significance, or the potential meaning, of your spending time with your new friend, and what it means to them. They will be much more likely to project into the future, and feel threatened by the possibilities. This is one way being friends in the beginning is very important. As long as it is evident to your teenagers that you are just friends, they'll be a lot more open to getting to know this new person. As soon as you're sure this new person will be safe around your kids, (don't be too quick decide), you can begin doing relaxed, casual things together, such as going to appropriate movies, attending the kids sporting events, having barbecues, and going to the beach or the lake swimming.

If the relationship gets more serious, and you're certain your new partner is reliable, and everyone gets along, you can begin to talk to your children (without the partner around) about your feelings. This is a great topic for family meetings, and your date can be invited to join in on occasion, if everyone agrees. Be very careful about trying to live together or pressuring your kids to like your new love. As much as you would like everyone to get along and to be as happy as you are, your children have a right to choose who they want to live with, and should have a say. If you make a unilateral decision, force the issue, or insist, you will make yourself and everyone else miserable.

- *Adult Children:* If your children are grown, hopefully they'll be generous enough to care about your happiness, and support your search process from the beginning. But, that is not always the case. Adult children sometimes have a problem with the idea of a parent dating. This is especially true if your former spouse, their other parent, has died, because it's difficult to think of replacing a parent who has passed on. If you value the judgement of your adult children, and they are worried about you, pay attention if they are negative about someone, just as you would if a dear friend was concerned. Find out what their reasons are: your judgement may be impaired by your emotional involvement. But, if you think they're just being possessive of you, you may need to ignore their objections. As with your teenagers, this will be easier if your adult children meet a new person as just a friend.

Whatever they feel, you have a right to expect that they will be polite and pleasant to your dates when they meet, and if you decide to deepen the relationship, they should make an effort to get along with your new partner. One major thing you need to consider about your adult children, especially if you remarry, is their financial rights. Keep in mind that, if you remarry and then die without making proper provisions, you may put control of their inheritance in the hands of someone who doesn't honor their claim. This is very unpleasant to consider, but as a counselor, I've seen a lot of terrible problems created by just this scenario. Before remarrying, get good, solid financial advice about protecting your children's inheritance.

Politeness
In addition to the considerations you need to make for your children, there are expectations and rules you should set for them. When it comes to your search, the expectations for your children are just extensions of the everyday behavior standards you set for them. No matter who they meet, your children should know the basic rules of politeness, how to behave around adult company, and how to treat an adult friend of yours when they meet for the first time. Your children should be able to meet a new friend of yours with the same social graces they use to meet your business associates, their new teachers, and other adults they encounter.

They should be able to respond properly when introduced, to call an adult "Mr or Ms", to use all the polite forms such as "please", "thank you", and "may I be excused". Children don't need special rules beyond these for meeting a date of yours. Ordinary politeness is sufficient, because your date should be treated as any adult friend of yours. If a new date begins to get to know your children in a more relaxed setting, he or she may invite them to use first names. If all goes well, and everyone gets along, the more formal courtesy will relax naturally.

Who Counts More?

If you are careful about going slowly and getting to know someone as a friend, your children will not feel pushed into the background, and they will not compete with your adult friends for your attention. Even when time is at a premium, your children should have enough alone time with you, so they can also enjoy being with your adult friends. As teens get older, if they don't feel threatened by your relationships, they will be more and more absorbed with their own lives and activities, and you will have more free time. Your adult friends are important to you, and if your children like them, they'll gradually become equally important to the children. Taking the time to let everyone become comfortable may be difficult when you're excited about a new relationship, but it will make a huge difference in whether everyone learns to get along.

Set Boundaries for Your Date

From the first, your new friend should understand how important being a parent is to you, and that dating has to take a back seat. If your date is also a parent, he or she should understand, and should feel the same about his or her own children. If you're dating a single person, this may be more difficult to get across.

Unfortunately, while your kids are still underage, being their parent can cost you a few relationships. If a person you find attractive doesn't want to have to face the responsibilities children present, then you will not get very far until your children are old enough to be on their own, off to school, or at least in high school and very involved in their own activities and friendships. You can still date, but it will have to be limited to your private time.

Your new friend should understand what behavior and language is off limits in front of the kids. If you're telling the children you are friends, you should act like friends: no physical affection or terms of endearment. This stranger should also understand and accept your need to make sure he or she is safe before introducing your children. Not only that the children are physically safe, but also that there will be no drunkenness, emotional outbursts, or other inappropriate behavior. This is where being with your new friend around others can save you trouble, because you can observe behavior for signs of addiction, immaturity, bad temper, harsh criticism or sarcasm, and other personality flaws.

Once you determine your new friend is safe, and introduce him or her to your children, times spent with the children should focus largely on them, not on you two adults. Having fun as a group is what's most important: not how excited you are about your new relationship.

As everyone gets to know each other better, and if things go well, your date can gradually be introduced to your household rules, family meetings, holiday celebrations, etc., with the intention of blending in to your family times as they are, and not changing them substantially.

All these rules will also apply to you if you are in the presence of your date's children.

Bonding with Kids
Bonding with the children should be done with extreme caution. If you met as single parents at a school function, and some bonding with each other's children has already occurred, then you must be careful that, if your dating does not work into anything more, that you can remain friendly around the children. Don't be overanxious about your children and your new date getting along. Take your

time, be very low key about it, and bonding will happen naturally. If you all bond successfully, everyone will gain from creating a blended family.

Be wary of bonding with your date's children, also, for the same reasons. If you are too quick to let yourself get close to your date's children, or let your date get close to yours, and the relationship doesn't work out, everyone will be devastated.

No Surprises
Do your best to communicate what your intentions are all along the way. If you want to make friends first, be clear about it as soon as you know, or from the beginning. If that goes well, and you want to deepen the relationship, make that clear, also. Don't make sudden big announcements to your children or your date. If you effectively, each new stage of your new romance and the relationship with your children will happen gradually; and you can talk about it slowly as it happens. You and your children can have talks about your new friend, and how much you all like him or her, as things develop. Your date and you can talk about how things are going between you, and also with your children.

Life offers enough unpleasant surprises on its own: you and your kids may have to deal with illnesses, bad weather, tough situations at work or. If you have to surprise them with a relationship development, either you're going too fast, or you haven't been communicating regularly enough.

Take Your Time
The buck stops with you, and that's where the toughest rules are. Because you're a parent, you must be responsible even if a new date makes you feel like kicking the traces and letting your hair down. You are the only one who can make sure that your new relationship is good for both you and your family.

You can speed up the time it takes to know someone is safe by getting to know his or her friends. When doing things in a group, invite your new friend to bring his or her friends along, and take the time to interview them. You'll be surprised what they'll tell you about past relationships, family history and job history. You can then compare it to what you've been told by your date. If it matches, and sounds OK, that's a very good sign. If you are not allowed to meet friends, be suspicious.

Careful, Careful...
Remember that your children are more vulnerable to hurt and disappointment than you are, so be very careful not to set them up. If your last relationship ended, your children's family life has already been disrupted once; don't force them to go through that again. Being careful means not only keeping your children, your home, yourself and your possessions safe, it also means making sure your children witness only healthy interactions. Being very sure about who you bring home will make sure you don't expose your children to witnessing hysterics, arguments, violence, drunkenness, rudeness and abuse. If this seems too cautious understand that con artists and sexual predators often see single parents as vulnerable and easy prey. Before you allow a new person too close to your home and family, be very sure you have checked the new person out. If the person is a stranger, and you don't know anyone else who knows him or her, be extra careful, no matter how charming, harmless or vulnerable the person may seem. In fact, too much charm is a warning sign.

Sex Is a Secret
Your children who are not adult should know nothing about your sex experiences. Part of your responsibility is to make sure they don't find out what you're doing. Don't take risks, even if it feels exciting: if your date values your responsibilities as a parent, he or she will help make sure you have sex at appropriate times and places.

If your relationship has developed to the sexual stage, you will already know quite a bit about your date. Make arrangements to be sexual at your date's home (if there are no children there). If you both have children, once they get to know and like each other, you can have them all stay at one of your homes with a babysitter, and go to the other home to be intimate. Or, rent an inexpensive motel room from time to time, or even get permission to borrow a friend's house while they're gone.

Keep in mind that you're demonstrating your behavior to your children. If you wouldn't want them to do what you're doing, make sure they don't witness it. When a relationship becomes a real commitment or marriage you can sleep together.

You Are a Parent First
You deserve to have a good time, to meet new people and make new friends, and you can do that with no problem for your family, if you plan carefully. Parenting is your first concern, and taking care of your children your first responsibility, but you don't have to be discouraged. Meeting new friends, as long as you follow the guidelines provided in the following chapters, can be a fun experience for you, your date, and your family.

To recap the guidelines already stated in this chapter:

Parental Dating Guidelines
- Make sure you know a lot about any new person before inviting him/her into your home
- Make friends before considering a romantic relationship
- Always introduce new adults to your children as friends, nothing more.
- If your children are old enough to have opinions of your new friends, listen to what they have to say.
- Do not pressure your children to like your new friend, or to spend time with him or her.
- Insist that your children behave appropriately and politely to your adult friends.

- Have regular family meetings with your children.

- If you want to get serious with a date, find out his or her feelings about children, especially your children, first.

- Gradually introduce a new date to your children by doing family oriented activities together. Give your children and your date a chance to develop their own relationships.

- Don't sacrifice your children's alone time with you to your new romance. Don't miss sport or school events in order to date.

- Don't share inappropriately with your children. Do not use them as confidantes for your relationship confusion or problems. Don't allow them to find out about your sexual relationship.

If you have the self-discipline to follow these rules, you will maximize your chances of success with your new relationship and keeping your family life going well.

Where to Meet Other Parents
As a single parent, you need to do events with or for your children anyway, so why not turn the activity into part of your dating research? There are a few things you need to be concerned about, but if you have the proper priorities, this can be an easy and productive way to meet someone who understands the issues of single parenting.

Child Related Events: Sports, School Performances, and Meetings
There are school functions you can attend from pre-school to college, and all will put you in the proximity of other parents, some of whom are single, and all of whom have children in the same age range as yours. Plus, you can often tell from the emotional well-being and the casual chatter of the child what kind of parent you're dealing with. Children (including yours) don't keep secrets well.

Your initial moments in sports, school functions, parent/teacher conferences, science fairs, and other functions will probably be absorbed by your child(ren). But, once the focus is on the event, you can get a chance to look around. If you're at a concert, play or sporting event or other sit-and-watch happening, you can strike up conversations with the people around you. Again, don't forget that even married couples have single friends, siblings, and even in-laws. As time goes on, getting established in school activities, and attending conferences and such as PTA, is not only a wise parenting tactic, but will put you in the proximity of other parents who care, and don't forget eligible teachers. As a parent, you'll find a great mix of teachers, other parents and students. You have the greatest excuse in the world to get to know the parents of your child's friends: it's just good parenting to know who your children are meeting. Depending on the activities you attend because your child is involved, (such as a play or band concert and rehearsals) you may have interests (theater, music, sports) in common with the other parents. So, by supporting your child's interest, coaching or scoring for teams, getting involved behind the scenes, you can automatically find other parents whose interests coincide.

You'll do best if you are pleasant, attentive to your own child and others, and helpful to the adults around you. As always, getting known requires getting involved, so begin immediately to volunteer for PTA Committees, etc. Find out where the suitable partners for you (i.e. single parents and teachers of the other gender) are involved, and get involved there. You can have great times for yourself and your children; and meet other parents, single and married, with whom you can form the village it takes to raise your children. You can get to know families which are safe and secure places for your children to socialize, and from where you have an excellent chance of meeting someone to seriously date. You could even meet a co-parent for your child, who understands parenting from experience. A date with someone from your child's school means your child (and everyone else) will know about it. Be low-key and do things with all the children, have outings and picnics and lunches as family friends. Don't date until you're pretty sure a relationship has a good chance, and even then be casual with the kids "Susie's dad and I are going to see a move that's too grown up for you kids." or "I'm going to escort Ginny's mom to her office party, so she doesn't have to go alone." Try not to show too much excitement to your kids. If all the kids like each other and both of you parents, they will be crushed if it doesn't work out. If they don't want you to get together (perhaps because they're still wanting their original family back, or don't want a lost parent replaced), they'll get rebellious and give you trouble. If the kids are already friends, interacting as a group as much as possible will give everyone a chance to bond. However, if the children have a falling-out, don't pressure them to get along; just wait and the problem will most likely pass. Children go through these things quickly and repeatedly. It's part of their learning about relationships, and has little or nothing to do with the parents' friendship.

Interactions between parents and children are very telling: If you get to know the children of the other parent, you'll know what kind of family it is before too long. If the child shows signs of stress, severe acting out, and/or depression, those could be warning signs about the parent. On the other hand, this family, like yours, has gone through divorce, desertion or death, and may be stressed from those things. As always, making friends is the best way to find out what's going on. Also, if you get involved in a school group, there will be useful gossip.

Be careful not to appear too eager to be close to married individuals of the other gender. If their spouses get concerned, you'll ruin your chances of entering their network. Rather, make friends with the spouse of the same gender, which will promote more trust. Any couple you get close to will be very eager to get you safely married off, and will work hard at it.

Networking Has Two Benefits Here:
1. You can get parenting help, trading off having children stay over so you and the other single parents can have nights off, for example. You can also find out from other parent's experience what works in terms of setting limits, discipline, parent/child communication, and home remedies for simple ailments.
2. You can evolve a circle of friends that includes resources for both your child and yourself, and will lead (through friends of friends) to meeting new people, and eventually the right person (who will not be a stranger, because your friends will know him or her.)

As you spend time with these other parents, you will be able to see whose interaction is healthy and supportive, and who has struggles and fights.

When you get involved on a regular basis in school functions, you can be found there, and it's valuable to exchange phone numbers with other parents of your child's friends. PTA and other school groups often pass out lists (with permission) of phone numbers of the parents involved, to make contact easier between meetings. Your personal cards will come in handy here, too. This is one of the safer groups in which to give out your phone and address, because of the accountability. Knowing that you are well-connected at the school means people will not normally behave badly; it's not a total guarantee, but it's a considerable protection.

Meeting someone through your child's school is a very good idea. It is easy, when your child gets to interact with other children and their parents in groups, to form a friendship, to see how the other person and your child get along, and to learn about the person's character and personality before ever declaring that you care, or letting your children know. If you go slowly, and it doesn't work out, your child hasn't been dragged through a bonding experience and then wrenched away from someone they're close to. You have a lot in common with another single parent, and you can benefit in many ways other than just meeting a partner. It's another can't lose situation. Of course, when you do meet someone significant, you'll need to work out co-parenting and blending family styles. That's what family meetings are for.

CHAPTER SIX

Successful searching

As long as you're going to all the trouble to look for someone to date, maximize your odds of getting the right kind of person. Most of your relationship problems can be avoided by finding and choosing the right quality of person to date in the first place.

Give Yourself the Best Odds:

People gravitate to certain places according to what is going on in their lives and who they are. Healthier places, places where something productive is going on, will attract healthier people. In places where people who share your interests congregate, the odds are better that you'll find people you'll enjoy. At nonspecific singles events and/or clubs, you'll find a bigger percentage of people with emotional and/or drinking problems.

Let's take a look at the right places. A new report by ReportLinker, a technology company that specializes in data, looked at how over 500 U.S. adults feel about (and use) dating apps— and not everybody is on them. They found that 81 percent of participants were not on dating websites or apps at all. Here's the breakdown of how they met:

- Through Friends: 39 Percent
- At Work: 15 Percent
- Bars or Other Public Areas: 12 Percent

- Sports, Religion, Or Hobbies: 9 Percent
- On A Dating App: 8 Percent
- Family: 7 Percent
- School: 6 Percent
- Speed Dating: 1 Percent

There's a reason why the breakdown looks like this. All the most successful places to meet are places where people get together for a reason other than meeting each other. The reason for being there becomes something you have in common. You get to interact with each other and know something about each other before you actually start dating.

Intrinsically Interesting Places with Good Odds

Intrinsically interesting places means things you would like to go to because the activity itself appeals to you, whether you can find people to date there or not. But, they also happen to offer good odds of meeting a suitable match. People in relationships, busy with work and personal lives, often talk longingly about all the things they'd like to do. "If I only had the time..." they say, and then talk about all the things they'd like to do:

- go back to school
- pursue a hobby
- try out for a play
- take up a sport
- get in shape
- learn to dance
- join a hiking/ camping club
- be a community activist
- volunteer

...and a host of other things.

If you have ever dreamed of doing some things you didn't have time for, now is the time. Think back to all the things you have fantasized getting involved in, and the suggestions that follow will help stimulate your thinking.

Attending Classes, Workshops or Lectures

Classes are natural places to meet new, intelligent and motivated people with common interests. You can find classes in anything that intrigues you in several venues: Local colleges and universities usually have community outreach programs for adults, in addition to their regular catalog of subjects. Municipal parks and recreation departments have classes in sports, crafts and other activities like yoga, dancing and tai chi. The Learning Annex (learningannex.com) offers one-session or ongoing classes, often with celebrity teachers. You can take classes in fitness, yoga, acting, musical instruments and performance, literature, great movies and countless other interesting subjects.

Opportunities for learning or exploring something new are the best places to meet desirable people. If you can choose something that genuinely interests you, *and* attracts the kind of people you're looking for, you'll have an excellent chance of at least making good friends; and a high probability of meeting someone suitable. Classes and workshops offer a better opportunity to interact with the other people than lectures do, unless the lecture is a regular event, or followed by a lab or a discussion. Dress conservatively and appropriately for the class content. Add a little pizzazz by bringing a very noticeable pen, notebook, purse, shoes, briefcase, apron or gardening gloves and hat. Here, you can get a little outrageous to offset your conservative clothing. An interesting scarf, tie, pin, cufflinks, smartwatch, lapel pin, earrings, can afford an opportunity to begin a conversation. Arrive a bit early, so you'll have some time to check out the situation before you have to pay attention to the instructor. Upon entering the class or workshop, look around to see who's there.

If the class has educational prerequisites, you'll know that all the students have at least that much in common, as well as at least a rudimentary interest in the topic. You can learn a lot about the other people here by paying attention not only to the subject matter, but also to the interaction between students and the teacher or lecturer, and among the students themselves. Who is bright, who is thoughtful, who helps others? Who has a good sense of humor? Scope out who's the most emotionally and intellectually attractive. Who seems to have a personality you could live with? If the instructor is single and the appropriate gender; pay attention there, too.

If you know a bit about the subject, be generous in helping others. If you're really new to it, don't hesitate to ask for help. Nothing attracts women more than a male in a cooking class who knows nothing and needs help. He'll be surrounded with solicitous women, and have a great chance to get to know several. Women taking auto mechanics or electrical repair can get more help than they could possibly use, and even offers to repair their cars. On the other hand, if you're taking yoga for the third year, and you offer to help someone else (with the teacher's permission, of course), you'll create a great, helpful, generous impression. Or, if you're a beginning student in a life-model drawing class, you can ask questions of the more experienced artists. It's flattering, and appealing.

This is a good chance to make a new friend, or even several, at class. You will be together, working on the same projects, for a period of time, a sure bet for making connections with your classmates. If you cultivate these friends properly, you can hope to be introduced to their networks, and find a special person. At least you're beginning with a common interest, in a positive atmosphere of growth and productivity. You will also learn something useful or fun, which may connect you to other resources for meeting people.

Be prepared to attend a few different classes to make it happen. Don't just sit quietly and hope for someone to come find you. While it could happen, your odds are much better if you talk to others, ask questions, or volunteer to work together on projects. Meet other students before or after class for meals or coffee, and if you're invited to a gathering of students at someone's home, make every effort to go.

In this setting, you have a chance to observe other people, which will tell you a lot about who they are. You can see them interact with others in the class, and you can get the feedback of others. When you find someone you want to get to know, use your interviewing techniques, introduce them to friends and later ask for your friends' opinions, and listen to your intuitive reactions.

When you've gotten to know someone in the class, especially if you've been for coffee and out in groups, a date will be significant, because you've had a chance to get to know each other. A date with someone you met here is more likely to be comfortable than a date with a virtual stranger; because you'll have a lot to talk about, beginning with the class topic and other people in the class, and moving on to more widespread and personal subjects. Also, in a class atmosphere, you can begin to see who's trustworthy and who isn't. Who can be relied upon to do the assignments and to fully participate? Who takes appropriate responsibility for his or her part in a project? Who is pleasant, cooperative and easy to get along with? Who speaks fondly of friends and family?

Church, Synagogue, Temple, or Mosque
If you are of a particular faith, the regular organizations connected with that belief are a very good bet for finding a potential partner. Even if you're not heavily invested in one particular faith, finding a generic Protestant church (if you're not used to religion, look for an Open and Affirming Congregation, they're more tolerant), or one of the more New-Age denominations (which tend to be more open-minded), such as Science of Mind (a.k.a. Church of Religious Science) or Unitarian Universalist, can be a good source for meeting people with good values.

People generally go to churches because they have concerns about being spiritually healthy, and doing good in the world. While some denominations define these terms in ways that might make you uncomfortable (for example, a heavily fundamentalist sect or a cult-like group), most of the mainstream denominations promote

146

excellent values. You may not personally like everyone you meet, and there may be a few bad apples, but generally, faith communities consist of people who get to know each other, and who can vouch for each other at least to some degree.

During the service, sit in the back of the room so you can see the whole congregation. You'll be looking at their backs, but you can still make some observations about the demographics of this community. What are the age ranges? Are there lots of parents and children? Are there small clusters of adults in your age group? (People in clusters tend to be single). Is it a large congregation, or a small one? You'll have a lot more opportunities to meet people in a large group, but it's easier to get to know people in a small one.

Dress conservatively, but comfortably. Once you get to know the place and the people, you can adjust your dress to match theirs. Get involved. At first, attend whatever gatherings they have after the service for coffee. If you don't stay for coffee, you won't have any chance to meet and talk to the members. As you get to know the group, find social functions or events to attend, or committees to join. Observe as much as you can during the service. Later, at coffee, you can begin to talk to people and ask some questions. Go to the minister, rabbi or leader, introduce yourself, say you are brand new, and ask to be introduced to some suitable people. He or she will know all the central people in the congregation, and will be happy to introduce you. Once that happens, people will feel you're a little special, and make an effort to talk to you. Don't worry about not knowing the faith. People will love explaining it to you.

If you like the group, volunteer to help with dinners, fund-raisers, cleanups and other events. Being part of the organizing or work committee gives you that golden opportunity to be in the company of others for extended time, focused on a mutual task. When you find a group with compatible beliefs and age range, you'll meet a lot of caring, ethical people who mostly have their lives in order. Some will be here in pain, looking for healing, but most will have made the religious observances a part of everyday life. Many people attend religious groups when their children are small. It's quite easy to meet single parents here, or married people who have friends they'd love to connect to someone from their church, mosque or synagogue. It's reasonable to expect to meet people who care about relationships, family and commitment. These are the values promoted by such organizations, and they fit nicely into your plans, if you want a lasting relationship. Church and temple-goers can get really excited about helping you connect with someone suitable. While it can get a little overwhelming, these are often experts who can find you the kind of person you really will like. You will meet a very high percentage of healthy and happier than average people. Research shows that members of such organizations have longer life spans, report more happiness, and have more lasting relationships than people outside faith communities. Plan to keep coming back, until you make enough connections to meet the people you need to know.

This is a *very* serious place to date, so do a lot of socializing in groups before you choose someone to single out. The whole group will be aware of your date, and any untoward behavior will be reported. This is a *community*, and if your date, who is a member of the community, is treated lightly or disrespectfully by you, there will be a price to pay in group feedback and censure. This works the other way, too, in that if you get to know the group, they will be equally protective of you. If your intentions are honorable, and the pairing just doesn't work out after a date or two, as long as you and your date remain friendly, there will be no harm done. So, you need to make sure the two of you are clearly communicating about what's happening in your relationship. Gossip, here, just as in a small town, will tell you a lot about the known history of any person you are interested in. It's definitely worth getting connected here: it will provide you with community support and the community gossip network, which are extremely effective in curbing and reporting bad character traits.

The structured nature of this type of group will help you a lot here. The spiritual leader (minister, rabbi, mullah, priest) usually knows a lot about the people here, and so do board members and other long time members, including deacons, cantors, choir members, Sunday school teachers, and everyone in the congregation, unless it is a huge mega-church. Once these people get to know you a bit, they will help you figure out who the other people in the congregation are. When you get to know the congregation, if you get interested in someone and either other members or the leader are less than enthusiastic about your choice, pay careful attention. A minister or rabbi may not be able to tell you some negative thing he or she heard in confidence, but may indicate non-verbally that there's something wrong.

Meeting someone here is a very good idea. The odds are maximized in favor of meeting someone with good values and getting to know them well before you have to make any commitments. You'll get other things by being involved in this community, also: a sense of connectedness, spiritual exploration, and a lot of good times.

Your Own Neighborhood
We often hear the phrase geographically undesirable and in places like Southern California, you can easily meet people at work, classes, or other groups, who live too far away to be easily accessible. It doesn't necessarily doom a relationship, but it's an obstacle to overcome. What if you could walk out your front door, and meet someone right there in your neighborhood? Wouldn't that be nice? Whether you can or not depends on the kind of neighborhood you live in. If you get to know your neighbors, they will trust you, and happily introduce you to their friends. If you're a young single in an established neighborhood with mostly elderly people, you have to network to see if any of your neighbors have eligible adult children, or friends, co-workers or other relatives you could meet. If you're a single heterosexual in a gay neighborhood, (or gay in a predominately straight one) your neighbors will be excellent neighbors, but not eligible for dating. However, like the

older kind of neighbors, they may very well have friends and family members who are eligible.

Knowing your neighbors can provide a lot: Safety, in the Neighborhood Watch sense, and instant pet-sitters or baby-sitters in an emergency, someone to keep an eye on the house or accept packages while you're gone. Neighbors who are talented at cooking, carpentry, home repairs, gardening etc. will give you free advice. Friendly neighbors can be a great help and a safety factor, too. If you're friendly with your neighbors, and the music is too loud, it's much easier to request them to turn it down without creating bad feelings. If there's a problem in the neighborhood, such as car break-ins, streets in need of repair, drugs, or an eyesore, you can all work together with your neighbors and city council to solve it.

Whether you just moved in, or you've kept to yourself in the neighborhood, you need to let your neighbors know you are interested in them. Pause outside to say a friendly hello, make a comment about the weather, ask when the trash is picked up, or what day the street sweeper comes by, borrow a cup of sugar, a wrench or a lawnmower, or pick up a piece of trash from your neighbor's sidewalk.... anything to get that neighborly feeling going. This is easier in a small town than it is in a big city, because in a small town everyone expects to know everyone else. Big city neighbors are often slow to warm up. If you live in a metropolitan area, your neighbors are the other tenants in your apartment or condominium building. You can get to know these neighbors on the rooftop in hot weather, or by the swimming pool, or near the mailbox. If you judge the building to be pretty safe, you can also choose an issue, like a broken lock or balky elevator, and put notes on all the other apartment doors about a meeting to work together to get the landlord to fix it. You may also meet your neighbors in local stores, especially the little grocery on the corner, or the mom and pop breakfast place down the street. Whenever you see a familiar face, smile and say hello.

Your neighbors can be almost anyone. Sometimes the neighborhood will indicate who lives there. For example, if it's near a school, you may have a lot of families with children. If it's an older neighborhood with individual houses, you may have elderly neighbors who have lived here for years. If you're near the beach, you may have students, surfer dudes or families with kids. Obviously, an affluent neighborhood means most of the homeowners and renters will be upper middle class or higher, and a low-rent district will attract people with less money, such as single parents and children, young adults starting out. A low-rent area will usually be more culturally mixed, with all kinds of people represented.

Whether your neighbors seem eligible for romance or not, remember how important networking can be. There might be a lot of eligible people connected to your neighbors, and if you get invited to your neighbor's party or barbecue, that eligible friend or family member might be there. If your neighbor has a warm feeling toward you, that person will have a favorable impression, too. Keep in mind, if you want to make a favorable impression, come outside (where you can be seen by the neighbors) looking good at least some of the time. If you live in a house, the more time you spend outside, gardening, reading in the sun or shade, and just hanging out, the bigger chance you have to meet your neighbors. Walking a dog on a regular basis is a great opportunity to meet other pet lovers.

If you live in an apartment or condo complex, then the pool or community room will work. The best thing here is to join the tenant's association, and help run the place. You'll soon know everyone and some of the dirt on them, if there's been any. If your complex has cocktail get-togethers, or your neighborhood has a block party, join in and socialize. Even if you don't meet your mate, you'll get acquainted with some other people and have more say over decisions that affect you, too.

This is an opportunity for friendly relationships with your neighbors, and a good support network; more help and more control over what goes on in the local scene. Possibly, some personal friendships, and maybe even that certain someone will come out of the network you create with your neighbors. There may not be perfect harmony. Your neighbors are the usual mix of people, some good, some problematic: so, you may have to learn the hard way whom to encourage and whom to avoid. Gossip will keep you informed. When it comes to couples, make friends with the person of the same gender, and you'll be less threatening to the spouse. Whether you find your partner or not, knowing your neighbors will be worth it.

As with work, if your relationship turns sour, you'll still be living next door, especially if you both own your homes. It's a lot safer to meet a friend of one of your neighbors, but if you do get connected with a neighbor, focus on friendship before romance. You can invite your neighbor to coffee at your house with other friends and neighbors, attend apartment complex gatherings, spend time out by the apartment house pool, get involved in Neighborhood Watch, and talk over the backyard fence; but take your time, and go slowly, until you know who your neighbor is. Take your time and get to know all of your neighbors as a group, to promote neighborhood (or apartment complex) events. There's safety in groups. Getting involved neighborhood improvement groups, Neighborhood Watch in cooperation with your local police department, cooperating with your neighbors in block parties and garage sales gives you a chance to get to know neighbors and become friends safely and carefully.

Don't worry about nosiness; it will really work in your favor. For example, if your neighbors know you through Neighborhood Watch, and they can see something unusual happening at your house or apartment when you're not home, they will report it and make notes about it. That can be a lifesaving or possession-saving kind of nosiness. Neighbors who understand when to call the fire department or the police are a huge protection.

Find out, if you can, who owns and who rents. If you own, and live near people who rent, find out who the real owners are, in case you have a complaint. Online sites like zillow.com can be a great source of useful info. Neighbors who are home or condominium owners have a financial commitment so they are likely to live in your neighborhood longer, and be more concerned about the neighborhood itself. Rental tenants are a lot more mobile, although there are many who live in one neighborhood for many years, and some owners who buy renovate and move rather quickly.

If your walls are rattling from loud rock music, and you know the owner of a rented unit, or the parents of the children who live nearby, all you have to do is call and hold a phone up to give the owner or parent a true idea of how loud the music really is. You'll get results right away. If you can't find a responsible party, you can call the local police station, and hold the phone up to let them hear the volume. You'll get a quick response. Getting to know your neighbors is a great idea, whether it leads to dating someone or not. It will enhance your lifestyle, increase your safety, and provide people nearby who can help in many ways, if you need them.

The Friends' Network
You get the best odds of meeting desirable people when you meet them through your friends. As you can see above, most people in successful marriages met their spouse through a friend or family member. Of all the intrinsically pleasurable resources you can have, your friends' network is the best. Friends provide support, companionship and comfort, and they also can introduce you to new friends. Getting together with friends you can count on, and meeting new friends or introducing your friends to each other can build a group with whom you can share holidays, good times, bad times and information. A solid network of friends provides a cushion and a shield in life's difficult times: someone to talk to

when you need support or advice. The same network will also make the good times better celebrating with you and congratulating you. There is nothing that feels as good in life as being surrounded by a trusted and trustworthy group of friends. More than anyone else, friends make your life's journeys with you, and know exactly how far you've come.

Rely on your friends' network as a resource. Even married friends know single people. It's not a good idea to get involved with someone at your own work, but people who work with your friends are fair game. If there's anyone interesting in your friend's office, meet a bunch of them for lunch or coffee sometime. Let all your friends know you're looking for people to date, and ask them to check out new friends you're interested in meeting someone. Introducing your new friends to your longtime friends makes a great character reference. Meeting someone already known to your friends eliminates a lot of worry.

Keep in mind that the friends you make will be very likely to have friends with similar values and lifestyles; choose the friends whose relationships (including friendships and family interactions) work very well, and ask them for introductions, or make an effort to meet their friends. Network with everyone you meet, everywhere you go, and make good quality friends and you will meet enough people to find a quality connection with a person you can feel good about. Take advantage of every opportunity to attend social gatherings with the people you respect and enjoy. Meet as many new people as you can, and be open and eager to meet their friends.

If your budget is limited, you can be creative. Reciprocate for formal dinners by inviting people over for a backyard cookout or payback for a restaurant dinner out with a home-cooked spaghetti dinner. When friends invite you to expensive places, invite them to someplace fun, like a fish cookery on the wharf, or a picnic in the park. As our opening statistics show, this is the most successful method, and has worked since long before modern technology existed. It is also a much more pleasant way to use your time, so once you start, you will be motivated; and have an excellent chance of success. In addition to being most successful, this is also the safest process, because whoever you meet through friends is known to other people you know. It is the safest method by far.

To succeed in networking, all you need to do is be a good friend, good company, and pleasant to be around. If you are an asset at a party or dinner because you can carry on a good conversation, the invitations will keep coming.

If you follow the guidelines above when getting to know neighbors, fellow volunteers and classmates or group members, you'll be a good friend, and you'll be popular, which will maximize your ability to meet new people. When you create a network of good friends, you can have a lot of fun. Your friends will share their favorite experiences with you, and you'll have a full, happy and rich life even before you meet a partner.

Work
The reason so many people meet at work is that it supplies the criteria for bonding: contact, with meaningful content, over an extended period: working together on similar projects over time. Statistics show 15% of people meet their spouse at work. Unlike online dating, and other one-time venues, the office gives you a chance to actually get to know and even bond with a person before declaring your interest. Working side by side with someone daily, seeing him or her under pressure, commiserating over problems and congratulating over wins gives you a portrait of the person on the inside as well as the outside. Because it's the inside that matters in a love relationship (despite all the media focus on the external) love can grow without either party really being aware of it. The couple develops a relationship infrastructure in an organic, natural fashion, as opposed to forcing it. These relationships often last a long time, because they're reality based. Unfortunately, the same ingredients can make office connections tempting even to the married, which is the downside of the issue.

However, although the opportunity to bond is supplied at work, the potential problems are an important reason to avoid looking at work for relationships. In today's more relaxed atmosphere fewer companies do have a jaundiced eye toward fraternization among employees; but a boss seeking to date a subordinate, or an employee who gets out of bounds, still risks a sexual harassment charge. But, even if those things are not operating, the problem of dating co-workers is what happens when the relationship doesn't work out. Still, many people find themselves attracted to people at work; it's actually an environment that's similar to the college environment, which is the easiest place to date.

The reason so many people date in the workplace, even though it's often disastrous, is that it's easy. You get to know someone well by working alongside them, observing them interacting with others, seeing them under stress. A lot of these relationships do work, and it's actually a good way to meet someone; it's just that the consequences of a poor choice are so big. That's why I recommend replicating those positive parts of office romance somewhere else. For example, in a non-profit group, a church, a recreational group, a political campaign. If you get involved in these pursuits, you can get all the advantages of taking your time, observing the other people, etc. In a voluntary activity, the consequences are minor, the rewards are great.

Office Dating Do's and Don'ts
DO remember that you need your job, and act accordingly

DON'T get involved with a married co-worker, no matter how much you like each other.

DO keep your in-office behavior businesslike: coworkers shouldn't be able to tell that you're dating.

DON'T share information with your coworkers about your dating situation. You'll become the subject of office gossip.

DO understand that, if the relationship has problems, you may wind up having to change jobs.

DON'T suddenly start dressing provocatively at work, it will alert your coworkers that something's going on.

DO remember your e-mails, phone calls, etc. are not private. If you must talk to your in-office inamorata, use your cell phone in a private space, where you can't be overheard, or talk in code.

DON'T allow yourself to be used by someone else in the office to get influence or information, and don't cuddle up to your boss in hopes of a promotion or raise.

Following these guidelines will make meeting someone at work, successful.

Special Interest Organizations
Groups that are already organized, with planned events and structure, can be extremely helpful, especially if your group of friends is too small or too far away to be useful as a resource for meeting new people. Organized resources, such as groups, clubs, churches, classes, and all the things we mentioned above, are available essentially when you want them, and provide the next best thing to a network of friends. In fact, if you attend meetings and events of an organization for a while, you will soon make friends there. Most people you meet there will be known to the others, which makes it safer.

A main objective of the Dr. Romance™ process is to meet friends, and find a way to be in their company long enough to figure out if you want to get serious enough to date them. Organizations with regular meetings or events give you an opportunity to be around the same people again and again, until you begin to know them. If you really like an organization, you can get involved, be on a committee or a board, and get even closer to the members.

Being in intrinsically interesting places works because you are enjoying the activity, and you have interests in common with the people. Being interested will keep you coming back, and having similar interests will make it easy to talk to people. Attending something interesting is much more realistic than going to a place solely for meeting people and finding romance. You're under a lot less pressure, because you're doing something you understand and enjoy.

When you're involved in something you feel good about, your demeanor will reflect that, and you'll be at your most attractive. The other people you meet there will understand your interest, and you'll have a natural and easy topic for discussion, that will lead on to other things. In this way, you'll get to know each other gradually and simply. The whole process is a lot more inviting and less anxiety-producing than singles events.

The people you'll meet there will often be mixed in age, backgrounds, marital status education and economic level, but that can be a plus. People who are not eligible for dating will be relaxed about meeting you, and they have friends. The ineligible people you meet might be a better resource for meeting new people than the event itself. Going to the first event or meeting may make you nervous, since you don't really know what to expect. You may worry that there won't be enough single people your age there. Don't let that stop you from trying a couple of different resources. Once you get there, you'll figure it out.

A special interest group is an organization, usually non-profit, which has a designated purpose. Joining such a group, or volunteering for it, is another opportunity to meet people.

1. *Hobby Clubs*
   Are you a collector? Do you have a favorite activity or interest? Do you love horses, travel, playing music, dancing, 30's memorabilia or a stamp collection? Are you enthused about model trains, kite flying, or model planes? Are you an avid skier, gardener or hiker? Do you love playing bridge, chess, computer games? Do you like the mental challenge of

math, or crosswords, or astronomy? Do you love reading mysteries or science fiction; or watching movies, plays, opera, concerts or sports?

Each of these activities has organized groups, clubs and related gatherings which are full of other people who are just as interested in your favorite thing. People here automatically have a lot in common with you, and beginning a conversation is easy. To find them, check your local newspaper, the Internet, or fan magazines devoted to your interest.

2. *Museums, Art Galleries, Historic Venues*
Every city (and many small towns) has many museums, art galleries and memorials, covering every conceivable subject. We are most familiar with art and history museums, but there are also museums for doll collections, trains, baseball, thimbles, and all kinds of famous people and events. The Revolutionary War, the Civil War and many other historic events, as well as prehistoric fossils, clothing, guns, shoes, inventions and various ethnic groups all have their own museums. Aquariums are like museums for fish. You can usually volunteer as a docent (tour guide), or some other capacity, and if you are interested in the subject of the museum's collection, you'll learn a lot and meet lots of other people interested in the same thing. Or, just attend some lectures or events at your museum of choice. This may be a source of classes, in which case the information about meeting others at classes and lectures applies.

3. *Non-Profit Groups*
These organizations are usually social and political, like Green Peace, The Sierra or Adirondack Clubs, the American Association of Retired Persons (AARP), a reelection committee for a politician, or a human or animal rights organization. Or, they can be focused on the arts, a school

alumni association, service organizations like the Elks or Moose clubs or organizations like Boy and Girl Scouts, YMCAs and other church and civic groups. Arts organizations, such as the Pacific Corporation for the Arts, a local Civic Light Opera or Community Concert group, or a Community Theater. Museum or zoo support groups or the local ASPCA may get your vote.

You don't have to join most of these special interest organizations to see what goes on and who's here. You can go as a visitor or a guest. Many of these groups are excellent for older people to meet suitable friends, since retired people usually have more leisure time to get involved. When you attend a meeting, go to find out two things:

1. Do you believe in the purpose of the group? And

2. Who is there?

Join a group with people you want to meet and make friends with. As you know by now, the idea is to make friends in whatever group you attend, and network from there. In these special interest groups, however, you'll meet people with strong opinions and passionate involvement in various causes, and you want to be sure you're comfortable with the cause and the people in it. When you attend, listen carefully to the discussion; and it will tell you about the attitude of the group and the individuals within it. At some of these organizations, members are evaluated according to contribution and dedication to the cause, while other groups are a lot more social and relaxed. That is why it is so important to observe the temperament of the group before you decide to get involved.

When you find a group whose cause or focus you are passionate about, you'll meet others who have that same passion. Out of that connection, you can evolve friendships and eventually a special relationship. Many excellent marriages have been fueled by a shared passion for a cause. But, you probably won't be comfortable with the people in a group whose cause or focus you do not share. Working together with people on a cause or project you are excited about can easily lead to a more personal relationship. The danger here is that the shared interests can blind you to the personal characteristics of the person you are interested in. Also, if the other people in the group know you're dating, that can lead to jealousies, etc.

As you work together with other people, especially if you're under some pressure from time to time, you'll get glimpses of the hidden parts of their personalities, and you'll learn who is trustworthy, who is vindictive, who has angry outbursts, or who's cooperative and helpful. Your personal cards come in handy here, too. If you are on a small committee, you will probably wind up meeting at people's houses, perhaps including yours. This is usually safe, as long as it's a group project. As time goes on, you'll interview, hear gossip, and observe others to gather information on what kind of people they are.

These groups are a great idea If you believe in the cause or content, and find people you can feel good about. Working together on a cause you are enthused about with people you like is a great recipe for making friends; and meeting people through friends is still the best way to create a lasting relationship.

4. *Volunteering*
    Volunteering at a theater or museum will not only get you involved with what interests you, it can save you money. Being an usher or volunteering to help backstage at the opera, concert hall, community concerts or local theater usually allows you to attend the performances for free.

Sometimes volunteering for sports (college sports, for example) will get you the same perks.

To add some meaning to your life, and to meet other people who want to improve their own lives and those of others, volunteering is your best bet. You can volunteer in the arts (be a museum docent, usher at concerts, build sets in a theater) in politics (join a campaign, work for an issue, join a human rights group, get involved in local neighborhood issues, if you're a senior, join AARP) in environmental issues (fight for a wildlife habitat, volunteer at a local nature center, join Green peace) for animals (join the local shelter, or an activist group like PETA); for your church, temple, mosque or synagogue; for children (at a group home, in the schools, tutor at your local library, help with scouting or sports programs); and many other opportunities.

Volunteering for a cause you believe in not only will enrich your own life, and give you a big return on your investment of time, it will also mean being close to other concerned people for long enough to really get to know them.

Less Favorable Odds

Dating Apps, clubs and singles events seem to be easier places to meet a mate, because we have been told by endless advertising, movies and TV sitcoms that they are the places people connect. Or, in the case of work, your ex, or therapy and recovery groups, the person seems easily available, someone with whom you're already in contact. It sounds like you can make a connection with Prince or Princess Charming without really having to do the work necessary to make friends and get to know people.

Making friends and going slowly sounds too hard when you feel lonely and/or desperate to have a new relationship, but they are the real way to end your loneliness and surround yourself with new, desirable friends, and eventually find your ideal partner.

Rather than being an easy way to bypass work, these so-called quick and easy places wind up wasting your time and money. If you get together with someone who has character problems such as addictions or emotional problems, you'll be in a painful situation of being bonded to someone with whom you cannot possibly make a relationship work. You can waste years doing this, and wind up so damaged by it that it will affect your ability to create healthy relationships. That's a terrible price to pay to avoid a little planning and effort. If you want someone to trust, learn to be trustworthy yourself. If you really want to be in charge of making good decisions, don't drink alcohol, and keep your goals firmly in mind. Better yet, bring a friend or two whom you *know* you can trust. Designate a driver, and go home with the same friends. If you meet someone, get your friends' opinions on whether the person seems OK.

Even at the places with bad odds, there are things you can do to make your chances better and your process more effective. Even though I strongly advise you to stick mostly with the places in which you will have better odds, I will cover as many possible venues as I can in the following guidelines, so you'll know what to do wherever you are to maximize your odds of success.

Dating Apps and Matchmaking Websites or Groups

While 7% of couples met on dating apps, this doesn't tell the whole story. I know a few couples who met that way, but while they love to tell the romantic story of getting connected through an app, they don't mention all the disasters they encountered along the way. Dating apps and websites are advertising, and about as truthful. People inflate their profiles, stage pictures, and flat-out lie at times. You have no way of really knowing whom you're meeting. If you're using an app or website, I recommend going very slowly, getting to know the other person via texting, emails and phone before meeting, then meeting in a public place. Definitely do an Internet search, check out Instagram, Facebook and other sites the person may have. You can learn a lot from things they and their friends post. I know a few couples who actually met via a dating website or app, some of whom have come to me for couples counseling. I know no one had a really successful matchmaking experience, and some had some really miserable dates. Others had no contact with anyone. The most successful site seems to be JDate.com, which is for Jewish people, and I think the success is due to all members having religion in common.

Matchmaking services can range from reasonable to very expensive. Your picture and bio can be viewed by other members who are looking for dates, and you can see their bios, and pictures. Often you are paired up by either a computer algorithm or a human matchmaker. Sometimes you get to meet people in person via a group at lunch or dinner. There is no guarantee of safety. The group acts as a clearing center for people who want to date, but it does not guarantee that anything you read or see about another person is true. Consider the questionnaire you filled out to make your bio. Is there any way anyone could tell if *you* lied, concealed a prison record or a drug habit? If they couldn't tell about you, you can't find out about them.

The bio and pic almost guarantees that this is about appearance. If you're not young and handsome or lovely, you are probably handicapped in this venue. If you are good looking, expect that to be most of what matters. People who are very physically attractive will probably get a lot of attention, a lot of dates, but whether it's worth your investment is a big question. Long before the Internet became all the rage, people found ways to use computers to find a date. Computer matching actually dates as far back as the late 1960s when companies began using computers to match data from hand-marked questionnaires. Today, it happens on the Internet.

Computer matching takes the information you give on your registration questionnaire, including facts about you and the requests you have about the person you're looking for, and matches to the answers given by other subscribers to the service. Once you've paid your membership fee, you can ask for all kinds of things in your match: non-smoker, within a certain range of where you live, physical characteristics (age, weight, height, hair and eye color, ethnicity) and the computer algorithm will get as close as it can. It's an automatic process, no humans vet the information, although some sites will block a member if they get complaints. When the computer thinks it's found a match, you and your potential date are both contacted, and then you can check out each other's bio. If you want to, you can send an e-mail, and begin corresponding.

Signing up for an online dating service is easy. Usually there's a smartphone app, which is free to download. You can find a website with any web search. Some things are free, such as looking at bios, but to use the full service, you usually pay a modest fee with a credit card right on line and join instantly. Then you upload your bio and picture. Costs vary, but you can find out via your Internet search. One plus of the Internet approach is that, as long as your relationship remains online, safety is not a big problem. However, at the point that you meet face to face, or perhaps when you give out your smartphone number, you must take the same precautions as you do with any stranger. The biggest problem is that days, weeks or months of e-mailing and phoning can make you feel as if you know a lot more about the other person than you do. Remember, no matter how sincere your new friend sounds, he or she may not be telling you the truth. There are a lot of documented cases of convicts or con artists putting up phone profiles to extort money from gullible people.

Your success will depend largely on the expertise with which you write your bio, the appropriateness of your wants in comparison to your own characteristics (that is, if you're 55 and want to meet a 20-year-old, you'll have a tougher time) and your picture. You must manage to make yourself attractive in print, not an easy thing to do. Again, most people will go according to your physical looks, unless your bio is so witty that it catches people any way. In a recent chat room discussion, people commented that the written medium means, spelling, grammar and punctuation count a lot. How well you write takes the place, to some degree, of your physical impression. So, if you're going meet people on-line, learn to type and spell, or get a spell-checker on your e-mail program. Be as positive, cheerful and helpful in writing as you would be in person, to make the same sort of good impression.

To increase your odds of success, send a good picture of yourself, preferably doing something you like to do. It helps if you have a website you can refer people to, because you get to tell a lot more about who you are on your own site. Search the web for services that allow you to list a link to your own website, if you have one. Find out if it costs extra, once you pay for membership, to contact individuals you are interested in. Find out how long your membership fee covers, and if renewals are the same price or cheaper.

Matchmakers are people who introduce people to eligible partners for a fee which is usually expensive. They advertise in every newspaper and magazine that has personal ads, as well as online; and they buy email addresses from dating sites. This is a profession with a history that goes back hundreds of years. If you sign up with a matchmaker, you'll fill out a form much like the computer match form, and possibly have a personal interview. They'll ask for your income, your physical characteristics and age, and other information such as your interests, habits (drinking, smoking), and education. Some matchmakers have stringent requirements such as ethnicity, economic level, education level or other requirements you must have to use the service. They will compare your answers with others, and try to match you up, and then introduce you. The big difference between a matchmaker and an online service is that there is usually a lot more person to person contact at the matchmaker, but it is also a lot more expensive. (Some matchmakers charge more for men than for women.) Search for matchmakers in your area; then call up and ask a lot of questions. Find out how their process works, what it costs, how many introductions are included in the cost, and how you will be introduced. Also find out if any parties or gatherings are included, or if it's matching only. There may or may not be some guarantees of how many matches you will receive, but of course, there are no guarantees that you'll meet someone you can create a relationship with. Every one of these services brags of their successes, but as far as I know, there are no reliable statistics on how often it works, (that is, leads to significant relationships) or whether it does at all. Before signing up, find out how other members would choose you, or you would choose other members, know exactly what information is given out, and what any extra charges are for meeting specific individuals.

When asking questions, be sure you find out whether the service checks the references of each applicant, and how much checking they do. Many such services do no checking at all. Your introduction could be to someone who has made up almost all their info. There are a lot of scams, such as mail-order mates from other countries. The usual cautions about meeting strangers apply. If the service has a place where you can meet a new person, use it. Otherwise, meet in a public place, or bring a friend. As always, follow the rules for safety from Chapter Two. If you want to meet the person one-on-one, choose a neutral, public meeting ground, which provides safety and an easy escape if the meeting doesn't go well.

There are several ways this matchmaking may not work out. First, you may not get any matches. In which case, ask for your money back (you may not get it, unless they give a written guarantee before you join). Or, you may get matches that don't work out when you talk to or meet them. If the matches you get don't meet your requirements, if you don't get any responses (or not a reasonable number) within a few weeks, or if the service doesn't live up to any of its promises. For your own sake, and for the sake of other people who may sign up, complain about anything that doesn't meet what they told you to expect. Businesses need to know they can't get away with false claims. If you have an opportunity to rate an app or service, do so. If there's a monthly charge, call your credit card company and cancel it and ask for a refund. They have a lot of clout with online businesses.

Clubs and Bars

The downside to these places should be obvious, but so many people think they're the place to go to meet people, that the myth has to be debunked. What is the reason most people go to a club? To drink, and to be around people. What does this say about most of the people there? That they're lonely and alcohol is important to them. Also, it says they couldn't find a better place to be, or better company to be with. While a few of the people may just be hanging out away from home, or meeting a few friends after work, but most of the regular denizens have some problems. While our statistics say 12% of couples met in a club, it says nothing about the nature of their relationships. If you don't want to bring a lot of problems into your private life, don't bring people home from clubs.

How do you behave in a club in ways that will enhance the possibility that you will interest the proper person? How do you know who the proper person is? I personally know people with happy and successful marriages who met in a club, but I know many, many more who found disasters. Walking in to a club can be an anxious experience. Before you even get there, have your plan together. Know what you're going to do, what you'll have to drink, (If you drink alcohol, I suggest limiting yourself to one drink, then switching to sparkling water, soda, fruit juice or even coffee), and what you want to accomplish on your first visit. When you walk in: Stop. Look around. Find a comfortable place, and sit for a while just to look around. What you want to look at is who is here. Sit back and plan to spend some time looking around. If you really want to learn about who's here, you'll come back several times. Proximity works as well here as any place.

As you observe the people, see what you can tell about their education level, alcohol consumption, and their interaction. Get your focus off who's cute or physically attractive, and try to observe who is kind, polite, friendly and interacting well with others. While you're still observing, make an effort to look pleasant and interested in what's going on. If you began by choosing an isolated corner, once you feel a little more comfortable, you may want to move closer to where most of the people are. If anyone catches your eye, smile pleasantly. If anyone engages you in conversation, respond in tennis-game style, answering every remark with something that invites another comment. Smiling and talking to various people sends the signal that you are approachable. Also, don't expect that you can avoid the long, slow process of getting to know your partner.

Because of the alcohol and the expectations of club culture, a date here usually doesn't mean very much. It's an escape from loneliness, sadness, and real life. Meeting someone in a club has a tendency to lead to instant sexual contact, which can derail any possibility of an ongoing relationship. The vast majority of dates made in clubs become one-night-stands. Expectations are set by the place in which your partner met you, and changing them isn't easy. If you decide to leave with someone from a club, be very careful... You're risking driving with someone who's been drinking, and being alone with a stranger. Both are terrible and dangerous risks. Date rape, traffic accidents and remorse are possible results.

Recovery Groups and Therapy Groups

Recovery groups are terrific places for healing, for finding support, for growing and learning. They are terrible places, especially for newcomers, for finding a relationship. Any twelve-step recovery group (AA and its offshoots) will tell you that; they strongly recommend you not date anyone in the group until you've been there at least a year. Why? Because people in self-help groups (especially the new members) are there to recover from various kinds of addiction and dysfunction, and they're in no condition to begin a healthy relationship until they've completed their healing work.

If you go to such a group and you don't need it, you're there under false pretenses, and misrepresenting yourself. If you're there because you do need it, you shouldn't be looking for a relationship. If you've been in recovery for a long time, and you are in an advanced stage of recovery, then you already know whether there is anyone else in the group stable enough to be a healthy partner, so it may be time to try someplace else.

The same thing applies to therapy groups. These are places to heal and do honest work, not to pick up on the vulnerable people there. If you're in a therapy group, and another member is looking very attractive, bust yourself by talking openly about it in the group, or privately with the therapist. Odds are, it's a bad idea. If should turn out to be a good idea, your honesty will only help it work.

Your Ex

The epitome of bad odds is represented by getting back together with someone who was a disaster once before. However, lots of people try it, so, if you're going to stop your search process and re-try with an ex, here are guidelines for improving the odds of creating a more successful relationship:

Dr. Romance's Guidelines for Improving the Odds with your Ex
- Go very slowly. If you're rushing into it, I can guarantee it's a bad idea you don't want to face the truth about. Slow down. If it's going to work, it will work better slowly, and you'll have a chance to build a better foundation than the last time.
- Treat it like a new relationship. Start from the beginning, and do it differently: If you don't fall into old habits, it could work this time.
- Analyze what went wrong the last time, and consciously try to do it differently: talk about it with your partner (your ex.) If you cannot talk honestly about what went wrong and what to do differently, you'll never change anything.

- Make sure your ex is as determined to correct the old problems as you are. If he or she is blaming you for everything that went wrong, disaster is immanent. If you're blaming your ex, it's just as big a problem.
- Insist on couple's therapy for both of you. Pre-commitment therapy can help you find out the pitfalls and whether you've solved the old problems.
- Consider seeing a therapist by yourself. Have an expert help you decide if you're dating again for the right reasons

Organizations for Singles

Wherever you are in the country, there will be lots of these: Advance Degree Singles (members are supposed to have college degrees); Professional Singles, Large Size Singles, Tree Toppers (for tall singles) Athletic Singles, and many other groups abound. Some are local, some are national. You need to sort through them until you find out what group suits you.

No matter how good the name sounds, you need to ask a lot of questions, and probably actually attend an event, to see which group you want to join. No matter how much they say their members meet qualifications, most of them don't check very carefully, and people can fudge their applications. To see if you'll fit in, ask for the demographics of the group: a polite way to find out the age range, income, attitudes, gender balance, etc. of the group. See what kinds of parties, gatherings or functions they have.

A group that runs activities with content, such as going to a play, lecture or sporting event, will be easier to relate to than a nondescript party or meeting, because it has a structure and a focus. It is easier to start up conversations with strangers when there is an event to discuss. Some singles groups are organized around having dinner, with about 6 people at a table, and everyone getting up and changing places between dinner and dessert, so you can talk to a number of people during the evening.

An Internet search will turn up lots of options, and often give you information about the group focus, how it works, how much it costs, and a calendar of events. Have a list of questions to ask such as:

- Do you have a membership fee?
- How much is it?
- What kind of events do you put on?
- How much do events cost?
- How many members attend your events?
- Is there are regular monthly calendar of events, or are they irregularly scheduled?
- What are the demographics of your membership?

Costs can vary widely. Sometimes membership fees are different for women and men. In addition to membership, the group can charge admission to events, and other fees. Be sure you know how costly it is before you join. Many of these groups, make claims about their success, but there is not much research, and most people in relationships don't report having met at singles groups. You're safe as long as you are at a group function, but as soon as you meet someone outside, all the rules of caution apply. Personal cards are essential here. Because there is little content here, you get very little chance to show your true personality, or see another's. To succeed, be friendly, outgoing, and socially comfortable. Smile a lot, use your interviewing skills and tennis match conversation. These groups give you a scheduled activity, usually on a regular basis, and if you go often, you'll get to know some of the regulars. It's a difficult way to know who you're meeting, however, and you might waste time you could be using much more pleasantly and effectively, doing something more constructive. If this is the only thing you are motivated to do, by all means try it. It's better than clubs, and it is something you can do with very little advance planning.

Internet Chat and Meetups

Lots of meeting rooms chat groups and bulletin boards exist on the Internet, separate from the dating services. These places have varying degrees of contact, content and conversation, depending on how they were set up. They can be x-rated, fantasy-based (you can assume a persona and an icon represents you on screen), intellectually challenging or boring and lame. Basically, they are just websites with software that assists you in posting a message, which can be read and responded to by others. There are basically two types of chats, bulletin board and real time. On a real time chat, other people must be visiting the site at the same time you are, to talk to you. When you type a message in the window provided, there's a few seconds of delay, then your message appears on the screen, like this (you choose a name when you sign up):

Your screen name: Hello, is anyone there?

If someone else is online at the site, from anywhere in the world, they can reply to you like this:

Their screen name: Hi, how are you tonight?

A bulletin board site, provides a similar window, but once you post what you want to say, it remains on the screen, and other people (also from anywhere in the world) come by whenever they want, and post a response. In 24 hours, there might be 20 posts after yours.

The best websites for meeting people are rated and given awards. By searching on the Internet for website awards, you can find the best sites. Also, once you connect to a site and chat with the people there, they'll let you know where the other good sites are. These sites vary wildly in character and are usually focused on a topic, like a lifestyle, so if you stumble onto a Sado/Masochistic, Polyamory or XXX rated site, don't assume they're all similar. There are many differences, and it's worth your while to check out a number of sites. When you find a site you want to try, you will probably be asked to register. It is almost always free, and usually requests your real name, your address, your e-mail address, and suggests you choose an online name and a secret password. You may choose your password, or it may be assigned to you.

Once you register and get approval, you have to learn to find your way around the site. There'll probably be a section marked FAQ or Frequently Asked Questions, and is usually a great source of information for beginners. There is usually a section called Introduce Yourself, and people who can help you figure things out. It takes a few visits to feel comfortable and understand what you're doing.

There are no statistics available about how many people meet in this way. I know a few couples who met at chats like this. Chat sites give you a chance to get to know people on a gradual basis, discussing all kinds of topics, before you decide to focus on one person. However, it is quite easy not to tell the truth on a chat site, even to the point of changing your gender, ethnic background, and education or employment. You may not be able to trust the person you're chatting with. Some of these chat sites host Meet-Ups which are events that happen in your area. Everyone may go to a concert or event with some way to identify each other; or meet at a wine bar or coffee house. Typically, people chat online for a while, move to private e-mail conversations, then phone calls, and finally to meeting live. The same cautions apply when meeting someone live. Go slowly, stay in public, meet with friends, and check out the other person.

Impromptu Meetings
Unless you live in a rare, isolated spot in this country, people abound in your life. However, you may not notice them. While it's a very big long shot, with terrible odds, you could meet your dream date at the Laundromat. As comedienne Judy Tenuta said: "It could happen." It has happened before. So, just in case, why not practice your conversational skills whenever you get the chance.

Quick!! You only have a minute!! What can you tell about the person in front of you in line at the grocery store (look in the cart) at the bank (look at what they're wearing) or at the Laundromat (notice what they're doing on their smartphone). This is a totally random event. You can choose the line you want in the grocery store, if more than one is open, but you often can't choose who is with you. This is where your observation and interview techniques come in handy. Find out as much as you can from what you observe and the conversation.

In these atmospheres where people don't usually notice each other, friendliness will stand out. Be pleasant, smile, be helpful (offer to help someone understand the machines in the Laundromat, let someone in front of you at the checkout counter.) Take an interest in the people around you and enjoy talking to them. All you can realistically hope for here is to improve your conversation and interview skills, and make your wait a lot more pleasant. Anyone you meet is likely a total stranger and you have no way of knowing about his or her character. Talking to strangers this way can be great fun, and you can develop skills to use in new situations, but the chance that a relationship will develop is very slim.

Travel and Special Events
It is not easy to meet people at special events, like concerts, festivals and shows, unless you get specially involved in a group, such as a movie appreciation class, a little theater support group, or a travel club, or a sports fan club or booster club. If you're just a passive spectator, you're as likely to be struck by lightning as you are to meet someone special. It can be fun to strike up a conversation with the person next to you, at your seat, or in line for refreshments, but the likelihood that the random seating will put you next to a desirable, eligible person, or that your conversation will continue once the event ends is very slight. If you're traveling in a group, on a bus, a train, or a ship, you'll have a bigger possibility of meeting a soul mate, but only if you get yourself involved. On a ship or on a train, you can be seated at dinner near eligible people (you can even

request that when you discuss your seating with the Maitre d'), but again it's only a random chance that you'll meet anyone eligible and interesting.

We've covered the major places to do your search in this chapter, and in the next chapter you'll learn how to make a good connection with the people you meet.

CHAPTER SEVEN

Making the Connection

Now that we've examined all the places you can go to meet people, once you've chosen where to go, how do you connect? In this chapter, you'll learn the skills you need for making contact, flirting, circulating and connecting on the telephone, online, or by text or e-mail.

First Contact: Generating Interest
No matter where and how you come face to face with someone for the first time, whether it's across a crowded room or right next to you, once you get noticed, you want to get and hold the other person's attention long enough to stimulate some interest.

The first thing to do is to make direct eye contact. Research shows that holding eye contact, even from across a room, is almost irresistible. Unless the other person is with a partner, he or she will eventually respond. Your gaze should be a little longer than a glance, wander away, keep wandering back. Each time your eyes meet, hold a beat or two, smile, and then allow your gaze to wander off again. You'll soon find the other person nearby, seeking to learn who you are.

The eyes have no equal, but if you're on a chat group or e-mail, a near equivalent to this first gaze is something that catches the other person's attention. Emoticons :-) or emojis, if handled correctly, might do it, or a signature on your e-mail with a well-chosen quote or quip like this one:

Oh, Life is a glorious circle of song
A medley of extemporania.
And Love is a thing that can never go wrong
And I am Marie, of Romania.

-- Dorothy Parker

The telephone version of this is a quiet, soothing, pleasant voice (if your listener has to pay attention to hear you, so much the better: being too loud on the phone makes your listener back away) and witty conversation. In fact, whichever of the above attention-keeping skills you do best could help shape your connecting process. For example, if you have great eyes, and a smoldering or inviting look, then organize your search process so F2F contact is how you begin. If you write well, then you might want to begin on the Internet. If your speaking voice is your best asset, move from emailing to phone contact ASAP.

Flirting

Once you've attracted someone and you have his or her attention, the next step is to increase the energy a bit by flirting. There are lots of attraction behaviors that influence people to respond positively. As we discussed in chapter 2, your body language is the first place to start. Make sure you don't appear shut down and closed off, and don't get a leg or an arm between you and your new friend like a barrier. Don't hug yourself, as if you feel afraid. Relaxed, open posture is much more inviting. If you don't know what to do with your hands, hold a beverage or toy with your watch or your jewelry. This minor movement will call attention to the watch or jewelry, which can provide a conversation topic, and it indicates you're a little nervous (rather than anxious) which makes the other person want to put you at ease. Most people think of flirting as happening in crowded clubs, but you can flirt almost anywhere, even with people you know well. Flirting can happen online, over the phone, by e-mail or face to face. Flirting is a way to let the other person catch glimpses of attractive things about you: your eyes, your sense of humor, your quick wit.

The other mistake people make about flirting is believing that it must happen between strangers. This is not true. You can flirt with anyone, whether you know him or her or not. Of course, picking someone completely inappropriate, like your friend's spouse, will get you into trouble. But, flirting is a great way to move a relationship from friendship toward a more emotional connection. Flirting with a person you have cultivated as a friend sends the message that you want to change the nature of the relationship. If you're following the instructions given previously, wherever you are, you've looked around to figure out who's here. If you're there for the first time, you're going to have to guess on a superficial basis. If you're in a setting where you know people a little, you'll have more to go on.

To begin flirting, you have to focus on one person. This doesn't have to be for the whole time you're there, but flirting is an invitation, an expression of interest, and to be effective you need to focus it on one person at a time. You can do this in person, online or on the phone. Keep in mind that you'll probably flirt with a number of people before you settle on anyone, so don't make this too important; think of it as a practice person, and you may be pleasantly surprised, but you won't be too disappointed. Once you have practiced enough to feel a little confident, choose someone with whom you have developed a solid friendship. Then try these steps:

- *The Glance:* The best flirting tool you have is your eyes. In fact, the word flirt originally meant a brief glance. If you're in physical proximity, keep glancing at your chosen person, then back to what you are doing, or around the room, then back to the person again. When you catch his or her eye, smile. After a few times, that person will know he or she is your target, and, hopefully will be flattered and interested.

While an inviting gaze, as if you're drinking in the other person with your eyes, is attractive, a staring contest is not. If you lock gazes, and both of you seem stuck, just move your eyes around the other person's face, or look at your drink or your hand to break the stare, and give the other person a little space, then, after a few beats, give him or her your full attention again.

- *The Approach*: If your interest is returned, in the form of smiles and glances back, but you are strangers, and too far apart to talk, try mouthing something such as "Hello" or "Nice Night." The other person probably won't understand, but will either let you know he or she doesn't understand, or will come closer. Often, men will move, and women will stay put. If you're getting an invitation to move closer, and you want to, go ahead. If the other person comes over, smile and nod your agreement. Once one of you moves closer, you can begin to talk a bit. Use your tennis game approach, and keep those eye-to-eye gazes going.

- *Animated or Quiet:* Flirting can be either lively and animated, or quiet and intense. While flirting always has sexual energy, tension and excitement, your personality and that of the other person will determine whether your flirting takes on a giddy, animated quality, or an intense, sotto voce (lowered voice) feel. Either one is fine, as long as you don't let anxiety get out of hand, and become too loud or boisterous. If you feel the energy rising too fast, simply quiet down and look the other person in the eyes for a moment. You'll feel your own energy re-focus and settle down, and so will your partner's.

- *The Conversation:* If you're good at putting extra meaning on words (subtly, of course) now's the time to begin. You can say indirectly flattering things like "suddenly, this party is a lot more fun." or, "I'm really glad I came here tonight." Imitate movie dialog for a couple meeting for the first time. If you're meeting this person at a place with some content, such as a class, a volunteer group, or a church group, you'll already have something neutral to talk about, which helps relax both of you. Your focus then should be on moving the conversation toward the personal. A question, like "What did you think about what the teacher said tonight?" Focuses the conversation on your friend's opinion, yet still relates to the content of the event.

If you're flirting over the phone, you lose the eye contact, but making little noises of assent: "uh-huh", "yes", "OK", "I agree" or "I understand" will let the person on the other end of the line know you're following with rapt interest. If this is online or through e-mail, you lose both eye and voice contact, so you must get your interest across in other ways. What you say becomes even more important. A sense of humor, wittiness and clever conversation are the essence of flirting. It's a way of letting the other person know that you're interested without saying it out loud. Flirting is an adult form of play; and a way to make a connection. Have fun with it.

Unspoken Communication
While you're carrying on your verbal conversation, especially if you're face to face, another conversation is going on behind the scenes. Your body language, the tone of your voice, the expression on your face, and, most importantly, your gaze, are all conveying messages of their own. Even if you're only talking about the weather, but holding each other's' gaze, giving a lot of non-verbal encouragement with nods, smiles, and little "uh-huh" or "um-hmm" responses (verbal nods), the excitement level of the conversation will gradually increase.

Over the phone, this happens simply with the tone of your voice and your voice cues. Those little encouraging verbal nods make a big difference in how understood your partner feels. If, on the phone, your partner ever says "are you there?" either you aren't holding up your end of the tennis match (you're not responding enough) or you are not giving frequent enough verbal nods. Being understood, desired and admired are the keys here. If you communicate interest and understanding to your partner, and you get a similar response, your flirting is going well.

If you aren't enjoying this conversation, and have decided you want to squelch the flirting and just resume a normal contact, simply remove your gaze (look vaguely over the other person's shoulder, or down at your own hands), let your energy subside, and stop doing tennis match conversation. If you give brief answers that don't invite a response, the energy will soon subside, and you'll be back to a normal conversation from which you can easily excuse yourself.

How to Speak Silently
Sometimes silence is the most effective conversational tool you can use. If you allow a silence to be there for a couple of beats, while holding your partner's gaze with a pleasant, interested, smiling expression, the energy level in your flirting will usually ratchet up a notch or two. Silence also allows both of you to feel comfortable with not having to have something to say every second, and produces a sense of restful familiarity. Too much silence, however, if you are shy or get tongue-tied, can feel awkward and jarring. Don't worry about a silent moment, but if you feel inhibited or stuck for something to say, just smile and say "I've just gotten a little shy." It's charming, and very attractive, and it doesn't force your partner to guess what's happening.

Suggesting Without Suggesting
Flirting is a meta-conversation: There's an underlying meaning to everything that's said. The surface meaning is, "I'm interested in what you're saying", and the underlying meaning is "I'm interested in you; perhaps romantically." Your exchange of meaningful glances is the medium for the underlying, more personal communication. If you like what is going on between you (especially if you know this person is safe, through the ways recommended in the last few chapters), now is the time to heat up

the conversation a bit. If you know how to play on words and use double meanings, you can move the conversation more toward the personal, and away from your general topic.

For example, your partner says: "I can get really enthusiastic about things I like to do."

"Oh really?" you respond with a raised eyebrow and a grin, "I'll have to find some things you like to do."

If this produces a blush, a return grin or a smile with eye-contact from your partner, you're on target.

The Tennis Match: Volleying the Conversation
In addition to all this underlying and unspoken communication, you still must keep the surface conversation going. I've mentioned the tennis match a number of times before, but it's so central to flirting and moving the relationship on to new levels, that some guidelines must be given here. Since flirting is about showing interest, understanding and attraction, demonstrating that you are interested in what your partner is saying, and want to hear more, is essential. Whether you're online, on the phone, or face to face, you need to keep your conversation going back and forth: what I call the tennis match.

Tennis Match Guidelines for Flirting
- Concentrate: Listen carefully to what your partner is saying; don't wander off mentally into what you want to say next.
- Volley (Respond): After your partner says something, respond directly to it, letting him or her know that you heard and understood what was said, and, if possible that you have similar thoughts or experience.
- Don't Argue: There is definitely a place for spirited discussion in good conversation, but be careful not to get too oppositional in this flirting phase. Your objective is to establish understanding.

- Return the Serve: At the end of whatever you say, invite a response by adding "don't you think?" or "What do you think?" or, make your response a question.
- Serve Again: If your partner drops the ball, or you run out of things to say on the first topic, offer a new topic: ask a question about something that was said before, comment on an accessory your partner is wearing and ask about it, or comment on something that's going on around you, and ask your partner's opinion.

If your tennis match goes on for a while, you'll learn a lot about your new friend, and you'll both feel you have a lot to talk about. If the tennis match is a struggle, and the other person isn't returning your interest, what you're learning is that you should focus on someone else.

Stealth Interviewing
Learning while you converse about miscellaneous topics is what I call stealth interviewing. Interviewing is just encouraging a person to talk about certain topics by asking questions. Professional interviewers do it with a microphone, and perhaps a TV camera, and it's very one-sided. Stealth interviewers disguise the interview in a conversation by answering the interviewee's questions, responding to his or her answers, and using the tennis match approach.

Interviewing techniques were explained in detail in Chapter Three. Practice the techniques enough that you can interview someone just by being interested in who he or she is, at the same time that you're flirting. Just pay attention to the answers, and take the time later to think about what they mean. When you're successful at flirting, the conversation will take on a much more intimate tone, and you'll get even more information about your friend's past relationships etc.

All these techniques: flirting, eye contact, double meanings, the tennis match and stealth interviewing sound like a lot to do at once, but you probably do most of them instinctively when you're interested in someone. The purpose of this detailed explanation is to make you aware of everything you're doing, and to let you know if you're missing any useful techniques.

Use Caution

If you've been doing all your flirting on the phone or the Internet with someone you've never met, you'll eventually get to a point in your relationship where meeting is the next step. Then, much to both of your surprise, you'll probably begin this flirting phase all over again on a new level, face to face. Be careful not to just accept that a stranger from the Internet is someone you know, just because it *feels* great. Anyone can tell you most anything about themselves on the net, and it's difficult to check. A major purpose of this book is to help you avoid problems online: While talking to friends via email about a column I was writing on cyber-relationships, and asking if anyone had experience, one friend emailed back. "Tell them to be very careful, there are many sleezebags online, like the one who raped my daughter."

Journalist Lindsy Van Gelder wrote: "'Joan' was a disabled single older woman who appeared on an online chat. She developed intimate relationships with other women, although never face-to-face. After several years, 'Joan' was discovered to be a middle-aged male psychiatrist, 'Alex'. Such online 'cross-dressing' shook up the many women and men who had 'encountered' Joan throughout the years, and led many to be more suspicious and wary of computerized interactions." There are many such stories.

If you're going to meet people on the Internet, or anywhere you're meeting strangers you don't know anything about, be extremely careful. Flirting online can be misleading, making you think you know someone well, when you actually don't know if anything you've learned is true. The flirt can go on for an extended period, and lead you to forget that the other person is a stranger. Anywhere you are meeting total strangers is equally dangerous. If someone toys with your emotions by impersonating the wrong gender, or lying about age, weight or financial condition, you're simply going to be disappointed and hurt. But, if someone conceals a prison record, fraud, or a history of sexual offenses, spousal abuse or worse, you could be in danger. Wherever you're meeting new people, follow all the precautions in this book, and never trust anyone you haven't checked out. This is the main reason to meet people at places where you can get to know them and see them in relationship to other people.

Circulating: How to Stand out in the Crowd

If you're in a group situation, at a party, a club, a singles gathering or a church picnic, you need to find a way to connect with several of the people there; meeting as many people as possible gives you more chances to find the people you want to know. Don't go to a group event and then stay in a corner with friends you already know. Get out and circulate! Here are some good ways to do it.

A Host is Your Opportunity

If you're in a setting with a host or hostess, you have a natural ally and helper. A knowledgeable host intentionally moves through a party, helping people to connect and enjoy each other. If you're looking for eligible people, and you let your host or hostess know, you'll be introduced to whoever's there and appropriate. This way, a lot of the effort is made easy for you. If you ask your host (before the party) to introduce you to single friends, you'll be introduced around the entire party. Your host or hostess may even invite some people specially to meet you. Being circulated by the central person of the gathering is not only easy, but enhances your status, and makes it easier for others to remember you.

Get in the Center

Being in the center of things makes it easier to meet more people and catch someone's eye. If you're at a party or a singles event, volunteer to help with the drinks or the food table, or to greet people at the door. If you're in a club setting, sit in the center of the room, near whatever the action is: the dance floor, the pool table, the music. If you position yourself well, you'll be in the center of a stream of people, and able to scan the crowd, smile, and catch the eye of anyone you want. At a class or other event, speak up, ask questions, and center yourself in everyone's attention.

Move

Another way to see who's at a party or gathering is to circulate through the room. This is especially effective if you know some of the people there and can say "Hi" to several people as you go by. Stop and chat here and there, and smile at everyone you pass. Survey the room as you walk through, noticing where the people are that you might want to single out later. As you pass, give that person or those people a bit longer glance, smile and nod. When you come back to chat with that person later, you'll have established a pleasant expectation, which will make flirting easier.

Making a Connection

Getting to know someone to the point where you want to date each other begins with making a connection. If you've been getting to know people in this group over a period of time, then connecting with someone on this particular occasion will be easy. When you circulate through a group or party, or you position yourself in the center so the people move past you, or even if your host introduces you, you need to be able to keep your new friend's interest until you get a chance to establish a connection. This requires conversation.

The Conversation, Spoken and Unspoken

While circulating, the kind of conversation you will have will be a bit disjointed because of the atmosphere you are in. People will be passing by, you have no privacy, and your surroundings are distracting. Keep the conversation light, teasing, humorous. Show your interest in the other person, but focus on simply making a good impression, and intriguing the other person enough to make him or her want to see you again.

With your attention and demeanor, you need to non-verbally give this impression: "To me, you are the most interesting person here, and I wish we had an opportunity to talk more than we can now." That means, your attention should not wander away from your quarry unless it's truly unavoidable (someone bumps into you, or speaks directly to you); and it should be obvious that you are listening intently and enjoying every moment of the conversation.

Your eyes and your smile are your main conversational tools here. You will probably be standing, so attempt to stand as close as you can without crowding your partner, look into his or her face, and, if possible, turn your back to the rest of the room. Stopping to talk to one person in the midst of circulating, or intentionally coming back after greeting everyone is a way to let someone know they are getting special attention from you.

The Tennis Match
When you settle down from circulating and decide to focus on one person for a while, you have an opportunity to use your tennis match skills; and the chaotic nature of the environment is going to make a smooth conversation difficult. Relax and have as good a time as you can.

Suggesting Without Suggesting
A few comments about how difficult it is to talk here, how much you're enjoying the conversation, and how much you'd like to talk more, should result in some agreement from the other person. If you get that agreement a couple of times, you can move to overt suggestion. If you're at a private party, invite your partner out onto the patio, or into another room, if one is available (such as the library or den) that has fewer people in it. If you're in a more public venue, suggest that the two of you go out for a cup of coffee either right after the event, or at another time. Until you move from this crowded scene, interviewing will be very difficult. Moving to another room or going out for coffee is a great way to get to know this person better. If this is a new person, move into making friends,

get together with friends, and follow the previous suggestions for getting to know someone in particular venues. Meeting someone while circulating at a party doesn't give you much of a chance to find out what you want to do with this person. To figure out what you want, you need to gather more information. You may be fantasizing about what you'd like to do, but the only way you'll *know* what you want is to get to know more about who this is.

Establishing Patterns (As this Goes, So Goes Your Relationship)
Research shows that people unconsciously look for behavior patterns to follow, and once a pattern is established, they tend to follow it without questioning. Each first event a relationship, starting with your first meeting, creates a pattern you are likely to follow, unless you become aware and consciously change the habits that are problematic. Doing what you've always done is easy, and it reduces stress when it works well. It is only when the old familiar pattern leads to problems that it creates stress. Planning your wedding, for example, creates patterns for dealing with extended family, solving problems together, making financial decisions, and being considerate of each other's feelings. Your first fight lays down a pattern for all future fights, so if you calm down, solve the problem and then make up, you've created a useful format to follow. These patterns are like the first layer of bricks in a wall. Every later brick will build on the pattern laid down at first, so if some of the patterns you've developed in meeting new people are not working well, it's worth the effort to learn to change them.

For example: If you should be tempted to wind up in bed right after meeting someone, remember you're leaving an impression that you'll go to bed with *any stranger you meet.* This is not a very favorable impression, so don't be surprised if you don't get asked on a second date. Going slowly, on the other hand, leaves an impression your partner can respect and admire. It's your choice.

Phone Savvy

Ah, telephone flirtation. It has all the comfort of being online (unless you use video, it doesn't matter what you look like, it's safe as long as you're only talking on the phone), and there's that wonderful feeling of being caressed by a voice. Why do you think billions are spent on phone sex and date lines yearly? The phone is a very sexy medium. The Tennis Match rule applies here. Whoever calls first then waits for the other to make the second call. If you've been given a phone number, it's natural to assume that means the other person wants you to call, but, unfortunately, it's not always the case. To get a phone flirtation started, you have to take a risk of rejection. Even if you want to increase the level of an established friendship to a flirtation on the phone, you may get rejected. So, alert your support system in case you need some sympathy, take a deep breath, and call.

If He/She Calls

If you receive a call from someone you're interested in, great! The tennis match rules still apply. Be gracious, responsive, and remember to toss the conversation back into the other person's court each time. Be careful to find out why the person is calling you, before you get too excited. You don't want to jump into animated, flattered, excited chatter only to find out he or she wants to know if you remember what s/he did with a credit card, or if you saw anyone steal a coat. Be glad to hear who it is, but a bit reserved until you find out if the other person wants to chat, to invite you to something, or to collect for a charity.

After Hello: Then What?

Before you call, have something to say. It can be a continuation of a conversation from a party, or an amusing story you found that relates to your friend's interests. You can call to let him or her know that something of interest is happening, such as a local art opening, jazz concert or lecture (This can lead to an outing or date, also). If you're calling a friend you already know a little, the welcome will be warm, and the call will be easier.

The first thing you need to do before risking a phone flirtation is to ask if this is a good time. You don't want to be intrusive. If, once you state the reason for your call, the other person responds by chatting a bit, you can use tennis match rules to encourage a longer conversation. Once past the opening exchanges, if you have established that there is time to talk, you can relax into a more free-wheeling conversation, and introduce some flirting. Laughter, humor, teasing and joking will set the right mood. If you have had conversations with this person before, and you found you have some subjects in common, return to those topics. If this is a call to someone you know from a class or group, finding a topic should be quite easy. At this stage, it is best to talk about impersonal things, such as hobbies, career, activities with friends, and interests such as movies, books, TV, the arts, national affairs, new science or technology, sports, and other general topics. Save more personal topics, deep feelings, spirituality, the nature of your relationship and sexual topics until the intimacy between you has grown.

More Stealth Interviewing
Use stealth interviewing techniques to find out what your friend enjoys, and what is interesting to him or her. On the phone, a conversation will often turn more intimate, more quickly than in person, because it feels safer and less intimidating when you can't see each other. Silence, of course, doesn't communicate much in the absence of any visual cues, and that, by forcing one of you to ask what it means, can also further the intimacy. Without visual information to go on, both of you need to explain more fully what you mean, which can work to further understanding and intimacy. If your flirting goes well, especially if it's with someone you already know; you'll find you both want to take your relationship to the next step.

The Next Step

After you have checked out the other person, gotten to be friends, and then raised the level of your relationship to a new emotional peak (and just enjoyed that for a while), your new relationship will begin to take shape. "If you really look, it's not long before you really listen, if you really listen, it's not long before you really touch," writes Rev. Denton Roberts, MFCT, M. Div. "and if you really touch, orders come from hindquarters and you have to make a decision." If you know the person you've been flirting with, going to the next step is wonderful. It you've been flirting with a stranger, it could be dangerous. Here's what you need to know:

Who is this?

Now that you've got your own and the other person's attention, it's time to make sure that this person is the kind you want. Review what you learned in Chapter Four about how to choose the ideal mate, beginning with who you are and who you'll need to compliment that. This is a great time to do this, because when you get caught up in the excitement and thrill of successful flirting you can stop thinking clearly. Remember, you must choose your new partner from the neck up as well as from the neck down; intellectual thought as well as physical/romantic/sexual excitement. This is when your old, dysfunctional patterns can take over, so take the time to think about this relationship, and don't get lost in fantasy. A little fantasy is fun, too much can spell disaster.

How Serious is it?

If your relationship begins to be serious and looks as if it might lead to marriage, you can save a lot of time, trouble pain and struggle by having *pre-commitment counseling*. An experienced counselor or pastoral counselor can help you take a more objective look at your relationship and any problem patterns that might be developing, and fix them before they become ingrained. As I wrote above, if your relationship lasts, whatever habits you develop in this time will quickly become ingrained. If you avoid talking about problems when they arise, it will become more and more difficult to talk about difficult subjects. If you begin here with power struggles, arguing, jealousy and criticism, your relationship can easily become locked in those patterns. However, if you strive to work together and build teamwork and goodwill right from the beginning, you can begin a pattern that will lead to a solid bond, and a love based on lifelong friendship and mutual caring.

In the next chapter, we'll see what happens if your flirting leads to a real   date.

CHAPTER EIGHT

Now You're Dating

Good dating is serious stuff. You're not just hanging out; you're seeking to find love. While fashions and fads and technology change, the basic skills of human communication, cooperation and commitment don't. A healthy, happy, lasting relationship needs the same abilities to share thoughts and feelings with each other, to work through problems with the intent of reaching a solution rather than just browbeating each other about who's right or wrong, and to hang in there, through good times and bad. What was true in Grandma's day is often still true today. Here's some old advice that still is valuable today.

What Would Grandma Advise?

- *Grandma would say:* "Why should he buy the cow when he can get the milk for free?" In other words, don't be too quick to have sex. This sounds arcane today, but there is a certain truth to it. When you have sex too soon, the power of that connection overshadows all other aspects. When you wait a while, and get to know the person you're about to be intimate with, see that person in a variety of settings, observe him or her interacting with other people, you'll learn more about the character of the person, and not be quite so susceptible to the surface attributes. This will result in a deeper and more meaningful connection that is more likely to last.

- *Grandma would ask:* "Who are his/her family?" We are no longer so concerned with class status, but it remains important to know your intended's background. Observing the way your date's family interacts will show you what good and bad relating habits your date learned from the cradle. While these habits can be good or bad, and the bad ones can be overcome, understanding family dynamics and traditions will give you insight into a lot of behavior that otherwise wouldn't make sense.

- *Grandma would ask:* "What kind of job does he/she have?" Many younger people don't realize that having significant work experience and holding down a job indicates a person has life skills. If your date is out of school and doesn't have a reliable income, it could be an indication that he or she isn't mature enough for a responsible relationship. If you just want a temporary playmate, this is fine, but if you want a partner you can build a life with, including savings, a home, family, and a future, take a look at date's financial habits and achievements.

- *Grandma would say:* "Never let the sun go down on an argument" I see so many couples who have long-standing resentment from arguments they haven't resolved for months or years. While it can be useful to take a break and give both of you time to calm down so you can reach an agreement, it is not helpful to avoid talking about things that are upsetting to one or both of you. Resolve things as timely as you can. Learn negotiation skills so you can solve problems together. If a problem is hanging around and not getting solved, or an argument keeps recurring, make a therapy appointment to get an objective opinion on what's blocking your connection.

- *Grandma would say:* "Don't give up. Fix whatever is broken." This is advice that I think is sorely needed in relationships today. The seemingly easy availability of other people to date through apps makes it seem simple to just let go and do something else. But no relationship is perfect, and most issues can be fixed. By working on whatever is not going well in your current relationship, you will learn critical skills, and if it doesn't work out in the end, you'll have a much better understanding of what you need for the next relationship.

Grandma's advice comes from long life experience, so heeding it can increase your happiness.

What to look for in a partner

As your dating relationship develops, if you are looking for love, you need to figure out if this person is a good partner for you. Here's what to look for:

1. *Good judgement:* is important because it means you can count on this person to help you make good decisions. He or she will be balanced and think clearly about whatever needs to be done. When you know your partner has good judgement, you can relax and trust him or her to do the right thing. If you can be trusted, too, then you have the ideal conditions for a working partnership.

   How to know: How does he or she run their life? Does he or she do well? Does she or he handle work well, and take care of business, pay the bills, make good choices? Is he or she wise about money? Pay attention not to how much he or she sweet-talks you, but to how thoughtful she or he is about life choices.

2. *Intelligence:* There are various kinds of intelligence, and sometimes those who have a lot of academic credits are somewhat lacking in the good judgement we just discussed. You want someone smart enough to work well with you, and to handle what life hands you as a couple, but academic learning may not be the only way to tell. Intelligence,

properly used, may help your partner to succeed in the world, and to make a better career. He or she may use intelligence to succeed as a business owner, and of course, there's the genetic heritage for your children.

How to know: It's not too difficult to recognize intelligence. Smart people usually do well in school, and in life in general. But it's important to realize that intelligence is not character. Good judgement and character are even more important.

3. *Trustworthy:* What you want is a partner who is honest and keeps promises. Someone who won't do things behind your back (unless it's to buy you a surprise for your birthday) Reliability, responsibility and accountability will give him or her the strength of character needed to keep marriage vows and promises. Dependability and Integrity are very valuable in a marriage, because they mean your relationship will be based on honesty and trust. If there's a problem that makes this partner dissatisfied in the relationship, he or she will be honest enough to tell you, and not just look for instant gratification outside the marriage.

    How to know: You can see honesty, dependability and integrity quite easily. How does your date handle problems? Can he or she speak up when something isn't working? People who cheat are used to taking the easy way out; they want to be liked more than they want to have integrity. Does this partner act like that he or she is above the rules? If he or she has unpaid parking tickets, or cheats on taxes and in business dealings, those are not good signs. Will he or she discuss a problem with you until it's solved, or walk out? Partners who walk out could also go elsewhere when problems arise in the marriage. If he or she was married before, why did it end? Look to the entire content of character, not just how much fun it is to date.

4. *Affectionate:* Affection is often somewhat difficult for some people. If your partner has trouble showing affection, how will he or she be as a parent? If he or she equates affection with sex, and cannot be affectionate without expecting sex, you might feel very dissatisfied in the marriage. Affection and kindness are the lubrication of a relationship. Being able to express positive feelings toward each other helps you get past awkward moments, recover from spats, and reassure each other that your love is still strong. It's also a vital characteristic for both parents to be able to express to their children. Children raised in a combination of affection and discipline grow up secure and with a strong and balanced sense of self.

How to know: The key is the ability to be affectionate in a way that does not inevitably lead to sex. While sex is important, and both of you deserve to have your sexual needs met, a partner who pouts if affection doesn't lead to sex is emotionally immature. If he or she is reluctant to touch, to say loving things, or to be close to you in non-sexual situations, there may be a problem with affection. It's important to talk about it, in case you aren't interpreting the signals correctly. Sexual energy is highest in the dating stage. But, if there's no affection, your relationship is not likely to do well.

5. *Financially Responsible:* This is very important, because financial irresponsibility, whether on the part of the woman or the man, will create life-long stress and deprivation. If your date gambles, spends money on drugs or even just the latest tech toys, or you overspend, your relationship will be in big financial trouble. Running up big debts on credit cards, paying too much for luxury items or houses, (or the wedding) can lead to life-altering problems. A marriage or living together relationship is actually a business as well as a romantic arrangement. Couples are supposed to have

income and expenses, and wind up with a profit, which we call savings and equity. Two grown-up partners, who can manage their money well, will be able to create the life they want, support their children, prepare for the future, and have some left over for fun. Good money managers live within their means, and are more concerned about whether their purchases are sensible than whether they're fashionable.

How to know: Look at how your date is living. Unless he or she is still a college student, she or he should have a job, an apartment or house, a car, and some savings and disposable income. You should have the same financial skills. If your relationship is becoming serious, you need to disclose your financial situation with the other. If either of you has a career that required a lot of expensive education, you should be paying down the student loans. Both of you need a financial plan when you're single, and should be able to talk about your shared financial future.

Reality Based Dating

I think most people are looking for love, partnership and companionship. If that's what you want, you need real results. There are basically two kinds of dating: One I call Hollywood Dating because it's based on romantic and phony media images and fiction. That's the one where you both have to be beautiful people, you go out as strangers, you spend a lot of money on a romantic date, and you fall in love forever. It's lovely in the movies, but it doesn't work well in real life. Then, there's the method I recommend, the get a life method. That is, you develop a social circle you enjoy and spend time with friends, doing things that are productive and things that you enjoy. If you allow this social circle to be large enough, you'll find plenty of people to date, and you'll already know what kind of people they are before you date them.

The good thing about old-fashioned courtship was that people got a chance to know each other before having sex, which can cloud your judgment, and make it difficult to make an intelligent choice of partner. If you're just having sport sex and don't want the relationship to mean anything, it's OK, as long as you take care of your health and safety. But, if you want a relationship that's enjoyable and lasting, you have to go a little slower.

If you barely know each other, then introduce yourselves to others as friends. If you have an understanding that you're exclusively dating (you should never assume you have this without talking about it) then you agree to say girlfriend and boyfriend or even sweetie. Save significant other or partner for when you have made a formal commitment. Just make sure you both agree how you want to be introduced before describing your date as any more than a friend. You have learned what cues to watch for in a profile, in conversations, how to protect yourself from fraud, and how to safely meet face-to-face. If you do connect with someone online, and the relationship develops, meet that person's friends ASAP, and have him or her meet your friends. Start with group activities, and don't begin by being alone together too much. A con artist can easily fool you one-on-one, but will have a harder time in a group, and the group will guard your safety. You'll get to see the grittier aspects of your date's personality when you share group activities, especially if they are challenging. If you think something you say will ruin the relationship, then screw it up right away: you want to know if you two can work through difficulties.

The Power of Self Control: Setting Boundaries

Before you go on this date, make sure you are in agreement with yourself. You don't want to be caught fighting with yourself over a decision when you need to make one. Decide in advance what behaviors and situations will be acceptable to you and what won't. As long as you are comfortable and feel these boundaries have not been breached, you can relax and flow with what's happening. But, once a line is crossed, you must be willing to take control of yourself and not just go along with something you find uncomfortable, unacceptable, or dangerous.

Here are some ways to figure out what your boundaries are in advance:

- Boundaries change as you learn more. In the beginning, however, set the line pretty high. If your new date shows signs of rage, drunkenness, hysteria, rudeness, disrespect (such as leaving you alone and flirting with others) recklessness, or other embarrassing or dangerous behavior, do not be polite or tolerant. Remember, your date is supposed to be on his or her best behavior, and if you tolerate this, it will only get worse. Many people do this backwards, excusing behavior they shouldn't, and getting hurt or upset later.
- Don't hesitate to leave if you must. If you're driving for both of you, tell your date you will take him or her home immediately. If you're not the one driving, tell your date you want to be driven home (unless the driver's been drinking too much), and if that doesn't work get yourself home by taxi, friend or family member, ride-hailing service, or public transportation. You need to set things up so you always have the ability to leave.
- Leave your date, male or female, at the restaurant, in a club, at a party, or at a movie, if his or her behavior is seriously out of line. This is the precise reason you need to be prepared in advance. If the date is your treat, leave enough money to pay the check, or see the waiter before you leave.
- If you stick to your limits on the first date, you'll find that your date will get the message, and either move on to someone else (good riddance!), or apologize and correct the unacceptable behavior.

Some of Limits to Set in Advance
- Your drink limit (driving and not driving)

- Your date's drink limit (driving and not driving) communicate this!
- Behavior limits (rudeness, social acceptability)
- Sexual limits (don't allow yourself to be pressured)
- Territory limits (not going to dangerous places)
- Distance limits (not getting too far from home)

Who Is this Date?

Hopefully, you've followed the advice to get to know your partner before dating; but, should it turn out that the person you thought you knew is too dangerous or bizarre or insensitive, be willing to change your mind. Even if you have been seeing this person in groups, as advised, you may, in rare cases, find that in private, with certain friends, or around alcohol, his or her behavior changes. No matter how well you think you know this person, be prepared to take care of yourself if necessary. This is the worst case scenario.

On the other hand, if your date turns out to be exactly who you hoped he or she would be, you can relax and have a wonderful time. If you've gotten to know your date as a friend first, the odds are excellent that you'll have a wonderful evening.

Who Asks, Who Pays, What it Means

In today's world, the customs about who pays, who makes the invitation, and what it all means are all in flux. If the old rules were just completely gone, it would be easier, but they remain in the background, especially for those who were adults when the changes began to take hold. If you have gotten to know your date before this occasion, you will probably have an idea of how traditional or modern your date is, which will make this much easier. However, if you don't know, the best solution is to ask. If your date has asked you out; offer to pay your share when the bill comes, just in case. If you are the one making the offer, and you want to share the costs, make that clear at the point of asking. Saying "my treat" or "I'll get the tickets" makes things clear.

You can keep your relationship on a more equal basis if you use the Tennis Match approach about paying, too. If your incomes or financial status differ, you don't have to invite your date to as expensive an evening as you were treated to. You can be more creative. A picnic, homemade dessert after a little theater production, a college ball game or recital, or a free gallery opening can all be lovely, cheap dates.

When you allow your date to pay a lot more of the time, you'll find there are resulting expectations. Be careful that you know what it means when the other person buys expensive dinners, orchestra row tickets, and sends flowers. Accepting such lavish attentions doesn't mean you have to go along with what is expected in return, but it can set up a very uncomfortable situation when you say "no".

First Impressions; Visual Messages
If you've made an obvious effort to prepare for this date, your clothes look good, your car (if you're using it) has been washed and vacuumed, and (if you suggested the evening) you have a plan and whatever is needed, your date will get the impression that this is important to you; which is exactly the image you want to create. Whether it's coffee out or dinner at your house, you can make an effort to show this is an important moment. Once you get to know each other, you'll both pay less attention to the outside and more to the inside, but for now, remember that your partner is still gathering sensory information about you. Look your best.

Preparation: Your Survival Kit
Because you're going out with someone you don't know well, and because the situation is new to you, be prepared for a variety of possibilities. If you put together a kit, a collection of the things you might need, and make sure you have it with you, you'll find it comes in handy, and boosts your confidence. Put a kit like this together once, and you'll always have it, not just for your first date, but for all dates and travel.

Money/credit Cards/ ID/
Hopefully, you've screened your date well enough that you can be sure he or she is reliable, but, just in case he or she becomes argumentative, hysterical, too aggressive sexually or otherwise, drinks too much or otherwise unpleasant, you need to be prepared to act independently. This part of your kit consists of some extra emergency money beyond what you think you'll need for the evening, a credit card, your identification, and a phone. Carry your driver's license and AAA card, if you have them. With these items you can always find a way to get home from where you are if your date drove or the car breaks down, or take care of yourself in any emergency.

Condoms, Toiletries Kit, and Emergency Supplies
Even if you're determined not to have sex on this first date (which is a good idea), it's better to be safe than sorry. Men and women should both make it a habit to carry condoms. I recommend placing a toiletries kit in your car. This kit contains your contraceptives, toothbrush, deodorant, shampoo, perhaps a change of underwear and maybe even something casual to wear in the morning. This may seem as if you're working against yourself, but if you have this kit with you, you're prepared to stay in a hotel if you get stranded somewhere, and it gives you more flexibility and freedom. Such a kit can double as a travel bag to throw in your suitcase for instant packing. Have a few necessities with you just in case. Women will probably have what they need for makeup touch-ups and feminine hygiene, but even men should carry a little matchbox-sized sewing kit (the kind they give away in hotel rooms, can also be bought at the drugstore), a couple of small bandages, some individually wrapped moist towelettes, a nail file and clippers, a pocket knife, and a comb. These items fit easily in the glove box of a car, but if you're traveling by public transportation, you can make a small enough package to fit in an inside coat pocket, evening purse, or men's pocketbook. These items come in handy in myriad ways, and make it unnecessary for you to endure an evening with a missing

button, a stain on your tie or blouse, or a broken fingernail. Also, you'll look very resourceful should your date cut his or her finger, break a nail, or catch a sleeve on something and tear it. They also double as instant packing for travel.

Safety Concerns
Know Who You're with: The more you know your date, the better your chances of being safe. If you've never been alone together, however, use some caution until you know how safe things are. Going out with friends is the safest way, if you know some of the group well. There is safety in numbers. If the entire group is known only to your date, however, you need to be cautious. Until you know how much the group is likely to drink, and whether there is a designated driver, you should probably drive your own car and meet them. Physical safety is clearly important. If you've gotten to know your date, and you keep your ability to think clearly, the following things are not likely to be problems, but until you're sure, here's how to remain safe.

Alcohol: Alcohol is the greatest cause of violence, death and relationship difficulties. Over-indulging in drink is a sure recipe for disaster. Know what your limit is, and keep an eye on your date. If you drive, don't drink. If your date drinks, don't let him or her drive. If you want to live for another date, if you want your relationship to succeed, you'll do whatever is necessary to control your own drinking, and you won't accept a date's excessive drinking.

Driving: Riding with a complete stranger in an unreliable car can be terrifying. Your date can be very reliable in every area, yet reckless behind the wheel. Don't agree to a date that requires a long drive until you know what a short drive is like.

Lonely or Dangerous Spots: If your date has the poor judgement to suggest you go into a lonely or dangerous spot on your first date, refuse. There is no need to spend a date in a scary part of town, or miles away from nowhere. If your date wants to drive you somewhere and won't say where, don't go. If, on a later date, you do find some reason to go far away, be sure you trust the person you're going with. It certainly wouldn't hurt to have a cell phone with you. If your date is adventurous, pay close attention, and don't be led into doing things that are too dangerous.

Your Place or Mine? It is very common for people to ask you out in order to case your home for a possible later theft. If you are wearing expensive clothes and jewelry or watch when you meet your new date, he or she may romance you to get close to your assets, not your heart. Be careful. Inviting a virtual stranger into your home, or going to his or her home, is not a good idea. You could be setting yourself up for robbery, date rape, or just a difficult time extricating yourself from an uncomfortable situation. If you know your date well, have made friends first, and spent time in group situations, you may have already been in each other's homes, and the decision to go there is a much easier one. Whose place you decide to go to, and when, will depend on many circumstances. The easiest way to do it is for one of you to invite the other over for dinner, or to watch a movie, the Academy Awards or Monday Night Football. Keep in mind that being in a date's home, unless there are roommates, children, or other people present, is usually interpreted by at least one of you to be an opportunity to have sex. If you have any doubts, talk about expectations beforehand. This is especially essential if you have children at home.

Your Children: If you have children, the necessity for caution is especially strong. As we emphasized in Chapter Five, your sexual relationships should not be obvious to your children, and you must behave very conservatively in front of them with your date. Remember, when you bring a date home, your children are vulnerable. They will be exposed to your date's behavior and attitudes. Their safety depends on your judgement and caution.

Sexual Safety: Sexual safety is a critical issue in modern times. In Chapter Two, we discussed sexually transmitted diseases, and what to do to prevent them. Even on the first date, when you don't expect to have sex, you should be prepared with condoms. More important is to be prepared for what may happen.

1. Talk about it ASAP: Whatever your concerns about sex, before you get to the point where you're doing it, you should talk with your date about it. This needn't come up on the first date, unless you're feeling that there are expectations you want to confront. This is a prototype problem for you to solve with your date. If you can be intimate enough to have sex, you can be close enough to talk openly about your expectations, your wants and your boundaries about sex. If your rule is not to have sex on the first date, and your date seems to be leaning in that direction (for example, asking you in for a drink), talk about it right away.

2. When is it OK? Know your own thoughts about when it's OK to have sex, and what it means. If you can be casual about sex, and not get bonded, how soon you have sex will be a lot easier decision than if it means you expect monogamy and bonding. Understand that having sex on the first date makes it much more likely that there will not be a second date. Although some people do follow through after a one-night-stand, the phrase exists because most people don't take a relationship seriously if sex happens too soon. "[Miss Manners] would have to spell out what the term 'one-night-stand' meant," writes etiquette expert Judith Martin "and explain that no, dear, she could not chastise a participant for not calling and sending flowers the next day, because these gestures had to do with another, unrelated social form called courtship."

3. What Are Your Rules about Sex with a New Partner?
   • No sex with anyone else?
   • Use safe sex techniques?
   • Both of you to be tested for STD's before becoming sexual?

- Do you have rules about conduct in front of your children?
- What about conduct in front of friends or family?
- What about steamy phone calls at work?

Before you have sex with your date, whether on the first date or later, make sure both of you understand each other's sexual expectations

4. Where? The other ground rules you may need to establish about sex is where it is likely to happen, although it may be premature for the first date. If you or your date have roommates, live with parents or children, or live in a close-knit neighborhood where your neighbors will notice an overnight guest, you may have some trouble finding a place to go. If you are uncomfortable having sex in your date's home, or in your own, talk about this in advance, also.

Other Dating Tips

Getting to the point of a first date is exciting, and energizing. Of course you should have fun and enjoy the moment, but if you get too excited, anxious and giddy, you might come on too strong. It's important that your anxiety not mask the real you. Keep your thoughts on the reality that this is just a first date, and you don't know what is going to happen to the relationship. Pay attention to what you are learning about your date, and allow the relationship to develop slowly over many dates like this.

Remember how powerful your smile can be, and use your eye contact and tennis match techniques to keep the conversation flowing. Think about what interests you about your date, and show interest in his or her opinions, experiences and activities. Be complimentary whenever possible, and respond intelligently to whatever is said to you. In spite of all the cautions and safety factors, you can keep your date light and easy, and have a good time. If you keep the focus of your attention on being pleasant, having fun, and not getting too far ahead of the relationship, you will be great company.

You can talk about anything, including your personal lives, past relationships and love in general, but don't be the one who brings up the intimate topics first. Be careful not to pry too deeply into your date's private life and secrets, unless the information is voluntarily offered. Keep your focus on learning about your date and don't get into talking too much about yourself. Dole out some information about you, especially if it relates to what your date is saying, but don't let yourself talk endlessly about your own life, opinions, experiences or activities.

Pay Attention!!! You Have Things to Learn Here!
The most important aspect of this date, in addition to having a good time, is to get to know each other better. No matter how excited, turned on or thrilled you may be about this date, listening to what your date says, watching what your date does and understanding how your date feels are still your primary objectives. One of the easiest ways to lose your objectivity and balance in this is to let yourself worry about what your date thinks about you. If you spend your time essentially trying to look at yourself through your date's eyes, guessing what he or she is seeing when looking at you, or hearing when listening to you, you'll miss what's really happening. It's a very self-involved thing to do, and it makes it impossible for you to relate intelligently to your date. What your date thinks of you is not really your business. You have a responsibility to pay attention so you know what you think of your date.

How to Avoid Dating Disasters
Here are some warning signs to look for. If you find them, be careful. No one is perfect, and the best of dates may exhibit a warning sign or two. Most of them are not fatal, and they may not mean the worst, but if you talk them over and work them out, you will find out how you deal with problems together.

Too Charming/ Practiced at this
If your date is not at all nervous, awkward and never at a loss for words you may be very impressed. Such a polished approach is very attractive and pleasant to be around. However, there could be a down side to this smoothness. It can mean that you're dating a professional dater; someone, unlike you, who has dated a lot, and is therefore very practiced and comfortable. This is fine if you just want to have a good time dating. But, if you're going to get attached, if you want a more meaningful relationship, or if you want a commitment from someone, this may not be the right person.

Angry Outbursts, Heavy Drinking or Emphasis on Drinking
If your date is able to drink a lot without showing it, that's a sign of alcohol tolerance such a person is used to drinking. It might be a warning that you're dating an alcoholic whose drinking doesn't show readily, but who still has serious problems. If your date drinks more than one or two drinks in an evening, or two glasses of wine with dinner; pay attention.

Out of control behaviors, such as rage (perhaps at the waitress, or while driving the car) too much drinking, talking about drinking too much, missing work, or being depressed can be clues about serious problems that can make a healthy relationship impossible. If you get such clues, be very careful, and go slowly until you have a chance to see if they really do indicate problems.

Control Freak/ Possessive
When your date has it all together: makes all the arrangements, can't wait to see you again, phones frequently, is intense and persuasive in discussions, always knows what he or she wants to do, sends cards or flowers, arranges things to perfection; it often feels very good, at first. It's so nice (especially if you're new to dating), to have all this attention, you may not notice how important it is to your date to have things go his or her way.

Jealousy can also be flattering, if your date thinks someone else is looking at you, or wants you to be exclusive right away, but it can also be a sign of emotional instability. That flattering interest in your attentions can turn in to a chronic lack of trust and suspicion. Controlling people are usually very smooth when you're only dating, and they don't feel they have complete possession yet. But, after they charm you into committing and bonding to them, the control can turn very unpleasant, and even lead to stalking or abuse. Be careful of the too perfect lover. What feels good on an occasional basis can be very oppressive when its every day behavior.

Signals of an Abuser/User
Anger, control, and possessiveness are all warning signs that your date may have a control issue, which can lead to abuse, but there are other signs to watch for as well. One of the reasons I so emphasize the tennis match approach to conversations, phone calls, and other aspects of dating is that strict adherence to that policy early in your dating will help you avoid getting attached to a user. Users are often charming, sometimes childlike, and usually appear to be somewhat helpless. Because they are so personable, it is easy to get sucked into doing a lot more than your share of the relationship work. We all want to help, to be caring and useful; but helping should go both ways. Until you know who you're dealing with, be careful you're not just being used. Users may con you out of money, but more often they just lay back and let you give more of the love, time and attention, until you feel unappreciated, drained and hurt.

Users are often narcissistic, a Freudian term which means they are so focused on themselves and their wants and needs that they aren't even aware that other people even have wants and needs. For various reasons, a truly narcissistic person has not developed emotionally past two years old, and is really incapable of empathizing with you or recognizing your rights, needs and wants.

Keep in mind that you and your date are both doing your best to make a good impression right now. Things will not get better later. They are likely to get more relaxed. If your date is not making a good impression, keep in mind that it may still be the best he or she can do, and make your decision accordingly.

Your Reaction: Scared, Bored, Intimidated
You may not realize it, but you have the ability to feel another person emotionally. This ability is called empathy and we are all born with it: it is how we relate to parents and others before we begin to use words and thoughts. If your feelings are at odds with what you think about the person you are with, pay close attention. Your body's reactions could be wiser than your thoughts. If you're feeling tense, stressed or physically uncomfortable, your body may be giving you clues. If the hairs on the back of your neck are raised, if you feel intimidated, frightened, uneasy, inexplicably uncomfortable, or any other feeling that seems out of synch with an otherwise pleasant dating experience, your subconscious might know more than your rational mind. Honor these feelings by being more cautious and going even more slowly, until you have a chance to find out what is going on. Emphasize group outings, and don't be alone with your date until you feel truly comfortable.

Lack of Friends or Social System
Beware the date who has no one in his or her life but you. Unless you've just met a person who's brand new to your city (or to this country), your date should have an active social life. Even someone who just came here should have an active social life back home, and be working to create another here.

No social life, no friends and not enough to do are all indications that your date has some problems relating effectively to people. While that can mean that he or she is at your beck and call in the beginning, it also can mean you will be expected to fill up your date's life, and that becomes a lot of pressure.

Tina B. Tessina

Sexuality: Too Much, Not Enough

Ah, sex: to be, or not to be, when, and how much; that is the question. Sooner or later in your dating, you will get sexual to some degree, even if you've decided to wait until marriage to have full intercourse. Cuddling, kissing, and petting are all stages of sexual contact, and will tell you a lot. If your partner wants to have sex when you don't its natural to be disappointed, but if he or she pressures you and gets angry, hurt or hostile if you say no, that's a warning sign.

Although it may seem overly suspicious to worry about all these things, it's a tough world out there, and being wise early in the relationship can protect you from being devastated later. Hopefully, in all these considerations, because you've thought about the serious issues in advance, you'll still be able to relax and have a good time; so good, that you decide to keep seeing each other.

CHAPTER NINE

Creating Happy Ever After

Because I see so much of the damage caused by people blindly connecting, rushing through the stages of commitment, and not creating the solid basis a true relationship needs, I always welcome the chance to do pre-commitment counseling. My job is to ask the tough questions that, in the excitement of a new romance, the couple may not have considered. Here are some questions every couple should consider before moving in together or making joint financial commitments:

1. *What is your definition of commitment?* Whether you know it or not, you and your partner will define your relationship. If you don't know what your relationship means to both of you, you risk repeating past mistakes, getting stuck in uncomfortable roles, or fighting about what a healthy relationship is. Talk about what you mean by words such as relationship, commitment, love, and faithfulness. You'll be amazed by what you learn.

2. *Have you discussed finances?* Next to sex, money is the biggest generator of problems, arguments, and resentment in long-term relationships. Couples tend to assume that money should be pooled, but it usually isn't that easy. A disparity in income can mean struggling about who pays for what, or whose income determines your lifestyle. Different financial habits (one likes to save, the other spends more, or doesn't

keep track) can become a source of argument. For many couples, separating your money makes things run smoother; you don't wind up struggling for control. You can split expenses evenly, or work out a percentage share if your incomes are different.

3. *What about household responsibilities?* If you're not yet living together, take a tour of each other's homes. Drastically different decorating styles, neatness, and organization levels can become sources of argument, and so can housekeeping and chores. If you have different tastes, it may require a lot of creativity and negotiation to decorate a joint home in a way that makes both of you comfortable. Additionally, think hard before moving into your partner's established home. You may have trouble feeling as if you belong in a home that was previously established by your partner, unless you participate together in reorganizing and redecorating it.

4. *How do you handle anger and other emotions?* We all get upset from time to time. If you are usually good at diffusing each other's anger, and being supportive through times of grief or pain, your emotional bond will deepen as time goes on. If your tendency is to react to each other and make the situation more volatile and destructive, you need to correct that problem before you live together.

5. *How do you show love to each other?* Sharing what actions and words mean love to you may be surprising. Even if it's a struggle, discussing how you give and receive love will improve your relationship. You will understand what makes each of you feel loved, and how to express your love effectively.

6. *How well did you discuss these questions?* Asking yourselves these questions are excellent tests of your ability to define and work out problems. Constructive discussion that leads to a mutually satisfactory solution means you know how to solve problems in your relationship. If not, get counseling before going further.

Staying together

The skills couples need to keep intimacy alive in a long-term relationship differ from new relationship intimacy skills, and they're not easy to learn, because people don't talk about them. Basically, couples need to lower their expectations of romance and glamour and raise the level of fun they have together

The most powerful thing you can do to keep a marriage strong is form a partnership, a team, where both parties feel respected, cared about and needed. Before moving into the deeper stages of commitment and relationship, make sure you have a clear idea of your rules and regulations for intimacy.

Here are a few suggestions:

Intimacy Do's and Don'ts:
- Don't try to develop intimacy with someone still in or fresh out of a previous relationship.
- Do discuss hopes and dreams.
- Do discuss your mutual hurts and fears.
- Do talk about what each of you want in a relationship.
- Don't assume having sex means a commitment.
- Do discuss sexual rules
- Do talk about what troubles you in your new relationship
- Do talk about what you like about this relationship.
- Discuss prior relationships as a learning exercise.
- Don't expect your partner (or yourself) to be perfect
- Do discuss problems that come up between you.
- Do discuss what you like and don't like.
- Don't rush things: allow them to develop.
- Don't accept or excuse bad behavior or rudeness; confront it.

Your personal rules for developing intimacy may be different from these, but take the time to write them down and know what they are.

Keys to a Happy Marriage or Relationship

If you've been following the guidelines in this book, you'll soon be focusing on developing a healthy relationship with someone you've gotten to know and been dating. When you're both ready to commit, these guidelines will help:

The markers of a happy relationship are: Cooperation/partnership, mutuality, laughter and affection. Keep them in mind when you're evaluating your relationship. Be on the lookout for early warning signs that things are getting a little off track between you two:

- If you're feeling resentful of anything; that's a definite warning. Resentment is like rust that can eat away at the foundations of the relationship. You need to talk about it, get it resolved.
- Arguments that won't go away and keep repeating are also signs of trouble.
- Companionable silence is good, resentful silence or hopeless silence (It's no use; he/she won't listen anyway) are problems.
- Problems with sex often indicate problems with other kinds of communication.

Some of the ways you can care about yourself emotionally, mentally, and spiritually are:
- Understand what you need to be happy.
- Don't dwell on the negative: if something's wrong, just focus on it long enough to understand it, and then change focus to finding a solution.
- Don't expect your partner to make you happy; that's your job. You can help each other, but you can't do it for each other; so figure out what you need, and then talk to your partner about how to get it.
- Count your blessings: no matter how annoying your partner may be at this moment, there are many good things

happening, also. Don't let the negative soak up all your attention.

The best ways to care about your partner are:

- Listen, listen, listen. The three most important words in a relationship are 'tell me more.' To consider your partner's needs, you need to understand them first. Listening does that. If you both know your partner will always be available to hear what you want to say, you'll be much happier. Knowing what your partner wants doesn't mean you have to give in instead, work together to find a solution that works for both of you.
- Resentment is dangerous to you and your relationship. If you find yourself starting to harbor little resentments, take care of it. Notice them, don't let them pile up. Talk about it with your partner without being accusing. You can own that something hurt your feelings or upset you without blaming; and your partner is much more likely to own up if he or she does not feel accused.
- Most of the time your partner doesn't realize how you feel until you say it out loud. Take the time to know what you want to fix the problem before you bring it up. Understand why you're hurt, and whether it's something that actually comes from somewhere else (like a previous relationship or your childhood) or it's something particular to your partner. Then, figure out what you'll need to fix it.

The most common mistakes couples make that drive wedges between them other than resisting and resentment, are:

- Not taking responsibility for your bad moods, fears and other feelings; and letting your partner feel responsible. That separates you.
- Not making sure you have time for your partner also separates you. Don't let TV, Internet, work, kids or other

people soak up all the time so you don't have any left for each other. Seek a balance.

When you feel like you and your partner are in a rut: you know you love each other, but you've just lost some of that zing when you're together, there are a few fun things you can do to freshen things up:

- Counting your blessings and sharing what you're grateful for can enhance the joy in your relationship.
- If you're bored, you've been lazy: get out there and do something together. A walk, a special meal (at home or out, depending on budget) perusing the photo album, a flower, a note; can all create pleasure and joy. Clear the calendar and spend a day just enjoying each other; including great sex. Have a date, like you used to. The zing will come right back.
- Dress for date night. Women don't understand how much guys like it when they have pretty underwear or are dressed up. He won't see your extra weight or your little wrinkles; he'll just see that you dressed up for him. He'll like it. And guys, she likes it when you clean up, too. For that date night, dress as carefully as you did when you were really dating.
- Learn how to talk over difficult subjects (money, parenting differences) so that they don't escalate into fights:
    o To talk about money, use your business skills. It's just math; take the emotion out of it, and talk as you would in a business meeting.
    o To talk about parenting, understand that there are a lot more ways to do it successfully than you think. Maybe you liked what your own parents did, and your spouse liked what his or her parents did; but you are two entirely different people, and so are your kids. It's great to find a book or parenting class to give you both neutral ground to talk about it. And you do need to talk about it. Each time there's a problem, solve it on the spot, but then talk about it afterward (without the kids around) to work out

how to avoid that problem in the future. Update your skills as your kids reach different phases (toddler, preschooler, grammar school, pre-teen, teenager, young adult) so you won't be always scrambling after the fact. Plan ahead together for the next phase. Take the time to enjoy your kids. Make sure they feel like part of the family by doing chores and helping out. Don't give them a free ride: it's not good for their character.

If you're having a problem you can't solve in a few days, consider getting a counseling session. You'll find it's very helpful, worth the money, and painless.

Ten things you don't know about marriage counseling.

As a marriage counselor/psychotherapist in private practice, I encounter a lot of people who waited far too long to come in for counseling because they didn't understand what it was or how it could help them. These ten things will clear up confusion and help you understand when counseling would be a good idea for your marriage.

1. It's not about airing your dirty linen in public. No good therapist will chastise you for your behavior or attitudes.

2. It's not about changing your partner. The best way to change your partner is to change how you relate.

3. It really can vastly improve your marriage, and make you happier.

4. You can learn skills you didn't know you needed, that will get you what you want.

5. It's not scary, it's enlightening. You won't be harmed or belittled: instead, you'll be delighted at what you find out.

6. It doesn't cost a lot. The earlier you go in, the quicker you can get the problem solved, and the less it will cost.

7. No topic is off limits. Whatever you haven't been able to talk about, the therapist will create a safe place for you to hear and be heard.

8. Fighting is not a necessary part of marriage, but communication is, and therapy will help you change your fighting to communication

9. Even if you are getting divorced, you can benefit from marriage counseling. If you have children, you'll have a relationship forever, so learn how to work together, even if it's just for their sake.

10. It's about partnership! Every marriage needs to be a partnership, emotionally, financially, socially and domestically. Therapy can teach you how to do this, even if you already get along.

Regular Meetings
You can keep the problems minor, the resentment level down, and the communication open, so that there is time and space for intimacy by making sure you talk on a regular basis. Having a regular State of the Union meeting increases your mutual respect and appreciation by. Here are two simple techniques you can use in all kinds of relationships: couples, families, even work partners and friends, to enhance your cooperation, tolerance and rationality, and to defuse conflict as soon as it arises.

State of the union meetings
Whether you are single, dating, married or have a family of your own, having a regular weekly meeting date to discuss the state of the relationship will make a tremendous difference in the emotional tenor of the relationship. If you're blending a family from previous situations, you'll find it makes a huge difference in your success.

When you have a regular chance to talk about what's going on in the relationship, problems, resentment and frustration don't get a chance to build. If you have children, every member of your family has a right to have his or her opinions respected. You don't have to agree or go along with what your child or spouse wants, but you should at least know what it is, and your child should know why you're overriding his or her preferences. Regular couple or family meetings, where everyone including the children expresses feelings, negative and positive, and all of you work together to solve problems, can help a lot.

Begin couple or family meetings as early in the relationship as possible, whether you think you have any issues to discuss or not. If you set a pattern of doing this early in a relationship, it will be easy to expand the group to include children if you have them. For relationships and families that are already established, it might feel a bit awkward to begin the meetings at first, but if you follow the steps below, everyone will soon experience the value of having an appropriate time and place to talk about issues and plans. Once everyone becomes familiar with the process, the formality of the meeting will relax, problems will be minor, and the couple or whole family can use the time for bonding, sharing stories and experiences, and creating quality time together.

Sit down on a weekly basis with your partner or family, and discuss everything about your relationship, positive and problematic, and how it's going for each of you. If you have small children, include them and get their input, also. Choose a time when everyone can get together weekly, and suggest to everyone that you order pizza, or cook something together.

Begin the session with a brief prayer or blessing, and a round of compliments, where each member gives a compliment to every other member: this creates a positive atmosphere.

Here are the steps to follow:
1. *Gratitude:* Each person states a positive thing about each person in the family, preferably something that has happened this week. For example, "I really appreciate how much you helped me this week when you knew I had a

deadline at work." Or, "I noticed that you made a big effort to keep the kitchen clean." Or, "Thank you for your sense of humor. It really helps when you make me laugh when I'm getting too serious." Be sure to thank the person after praising them. If you follow a religious tradition, you can open the meeting by giving thanks in the manner of your faith.

2. *Improvements:* Each person then mentions one thing they want to improve, and what they want to do to make it better. Small children will need help until they understand, but they will catch on quickly. Even you and one child can do this. The rule is that, in order to bring up a complaint, you must have a suggestion for a solution, even if you don't think it's the best possible solution.

3. *Problem Solving:* If anyone has a problem to solve, he or she can describe it, and then ask for help from the group to solve it. Everyone can work together to come up with a solution. Be careful not to allow the description of the problem to deteriorate into criticism and complaining. To state a problem, use matter-of-fact terms, and use I messages: "I get discouraged and frustrated when the house gets messy." "We need to come up with some money to fix the car." "I have a problem at school." "I need help figuring out how not to fight with Susie anymore".

This simple meeting will do more for the state of your intimate or family relationship than you can imagine. If you deal with problems early, and approach them with a team spirit of solving them together, most problems can be solved before they become disasters.

These meetings will accomplish a great deal, and can change the nature of what I call your relationship reservoir:

Your relationship reservoir

Every relationship (including those with family, friends and between parents and children) has what I call the relationship reservoir. Over the course of your relationship, the interaction between you: every kind or unkind word, every gesture of support or criticism, every honest or dishonest interaction between you, every gesture of affection or coldness, add up over the time you spend together.

If you fill your reservoir with good feelings, forgiveness, support, honesty, appreciation, caring, affection, emotional intimacy (and sexual intimacy where appropriate,) you build up a backlog of good will and affection; your memories will be warm and mutually admiring. If you fill it with coldness, criticism, ingratitude, dishonesty, demands, and dissatisfaction, you'll have a reservoir of resentment and disdain.

Each time your relationship makes demands on you as a result of major problems, separations, disagreements, illnesses, and stress, you will draw on your relationship reservoir. If you have built up a supply of good feelings and goodwill with your daily interaction, you'll cheerfully give what's asked of you. If not, whatever's asked will seem like too much to give.

I wish you a reservoir overflowing with warmth and good feelings: the true guarantee of a lasting relationship.

If you follow all the guidelines in this book, you'll have a better chance of being clear about what you do want, finding others who have similar reasons, and getting together with someone who feels the same as you do will be easier and clearer.

No matter what you're looking for, I wish you well and hope you find the perfect love.

About the Author

Author Bio: Tina B. Tessina, Ph.D. (www.tinatessina.com) is a licensed psychotherapist in S. California since 1978 with over 40 years' experience in counseling individuals and couples and author of 14 books in 17 languages, including *It Ends With You: Grow Up and Out of Dysfunction*; *The Ten Smartest Decisions a Woman Can Make After Forty*; *Love Styles: How to Celebrate Your Differences*, *The Real 13th Step* , *How to Be Happy Partners: Working it Out Together* and *How to Be a Couple and Still Be Free*. She writes the Dr. Romance™ blog (drromance.typepad.com), and the "Happiness Tips from Tina" email newsletter. Online, she's known as Dr. Romance™ Dr. Tessina appears frequently on radio, TV, video and podcasts. She tweets @tinatessina.

Dr. Tessina has been CRO (Chief Romance Officer) for LoveForever.com, a website designed to strengthen relationships and guide couples through the various stages of their relationship with personalized tips, courses, and online couples counseling. Dr. Tessina appears frequently on radio, and such TV shows as "Oprah", "Larry King Live" and ABC News.

Dr. Tessina's many years of experience in helping people shows in her writing. Her very practical books are filled with reader-friendly exercises, suggestions, guidelines, and examples. Although simply and elegantly written they are deceptively powerful. Each of Dr. Tessina's books draws on the knowledge she has gained in her years of clinical work with individuals and couples. Each book was written as Dr. Tessina discovered a body of information needed by her clients that was not already published. Her books are not mere speculation, but the concrete result of Dr. Tessina's experiences in helping people overcome their resistance, their fears and their emotional wounds.

In addition to her professional work, Dr. Tessina is a trained opera singer and a lyric coloratura. She also writes poetry and song lyrics (her songs have been recorded by several well-known singers, including Helen Reddy), speaks Spanish and some French, and loves ballroom dancing. She lives in Long Beach, California with her husband of 36 years, Richard Sharrard, ballroom instructor and owner of DanceFactoryOnline.com. They spend the little spare time they have traveling, enjoying their vintage California bungalow, gardening, and playing with their three dogs. Dr. Tessina earned both her B.A. and M.A. at The Lindenwood Colleges, St. Charles, Missouri (1977), and her Ph.D. at Pacific Western University, Los Angeles (1987). She is a Diplomate of the American Psychotherapy Association and a Certified Domestic Violence Counselor.

Connect with Dr. Tessina online:

http://www.tinatessina.com

Dr. Romance Blog: http://drromance.typepad.com

Twitter.com/tinatessina

Facebook.com/TinaTessina

Facebook.com/TheReal13thStep

https://www.facebook.com/DrRomanceBlog

Other Books by the Author

By Tina B. Tessina

The Real 13th Step: Discovering Confidence, Self-Reliance and Independence Beyond the Twelve Step Programs Digital Parchment Services 2015 ISBN 13: 978-1615089963

It Ends with You: Grow Up and Out of Dysfunction 2nd edition Muffinhaven Publishing 2014 ISBN-10 149733070X ISBN 13: 978-149733702;

The Ten Smartest Decisions a Woman Can Make After Forty 2nd edition Muffinhaven Publishing 2014 ISBN-10: 1494842033   ISBN-13: 978-1494842031

Love Styles: How to Celebrate Your Differences 2nd edition Muffinhaven Publishing 2011 ISBN-10: 1463783531 ISBN-13: 978-1463783532

Money, Sex and Kids: Stop Fighting about the Three Things That Can Ruin Your Marriage Adams Media 2008 ISBN #1-59869-325-5 256 pages, trade paper, list $12.95

The Commuter Marriage: Keep Your Relationship Close While You're Far Apart Adams Media 2008 ISBN: 1-59869-432-4 220 pages, trade paper, list $14.95

Gay Relationships: How to Find Them, How to Improve Them, How to Make Them Last   New Revised edition Tarcher/Putnam 2003. ISBN# 0-87477-566-3. 228 pages trade paper, list $14.95 original edition Tarcher 1988

The Unofficial Guide to Dating Again Wiley, NY 2002 ISBN: 0-02-862454-8, 385 pages trade paper list $16.99 (OOP)

By Riley K. Smith and Tina B. Tessina

How to Be a Couple and Still Be Free 4th Edition ISBN: 1-56414-549-2, 200 pages (co-author Riley K. Smith) Trade paper, list $14.95 Fumbled Book Press, Oakland, CA

How to Be Happy Partners: Working It Out Together Muffinhaven Press May 2016 ISBN-10: 1530583594 ISBN-13: 978-1530583591

True Partners: An Inner Workbook Tarcher 1993 Paperback: 217 ISBN-10: 0874777275 ISBN-13: 978-0874777277 (OOP)

Equal Partners: How to Build a Lasting Relationship Hodder & Stoughton, 1994 ISBN-10: 0340602775 ISBN – 13: 978-0340602775 (OOP)

By Tina B. Tessina, and Elizabeth Friar Williams

The 10 Smartest Decisions A Woman Can Make Before 40 HCI, Deerfield Beach, 1998 ISBN: 1-55-874614-5, 200 pages Trade paper, list $10.95 (12 foreign language editions)

Made in the USA
San Bernardino, CA
02 September 2018